Reality? Knowledge? Philosophy!

An Introduction to Metaphysics and Epistemology

Stephen Hetherington

D1447621

Edinburgh University Press

For Iqbal Masih (c. 1982–95)
There are too few like him. There are too many like him.

© Stephen Hetherington, 2003

Edinburgh University Press Ltd
22 George Square, Edinburgh

Typeset in Sabon
by Mizpah Publishing Services, Chennai, India, and
printed and bound in Great Britain
by Antony Rowe Ltd, Chippenham

A CIP record for this book is available
from the British Library

ISBN 0 7486 1664 0 (hardback)
ISBN 0 7486 1665 9 (paperback)

The right of Stephen Hetherington
to be identified as author of this work
has been asserted in accordance with
the Copyright, Designs and Patents Act 1988.

Contents

Preface

Do you have a philosophy of people – of our natures and capacities? What are we? Do we matter? What can we do? What can we know? A philosophy of existence is a *metaphysics*; a philosophy of knowledge is an *epistemology*. Can we develop a metaphysics of *our* existence and an epistemology of *our* knowledge? To do so is to create a philosophy of a large part of our lives.

What is a philosophy, though? Your philosophy of *T* (for some topic *T*) comprises your most basic views about *T*. They are your *guiding* ideas or claims or principles about *T*. There is some generality to them. Even if silently, you look to them when answering specific questions about *T*. For example, if we ask a Catholic priest whether some particular abortion is morally permissible, we know in advance that he will say 'No' – because we know enough of what the Catholic Church's underlying philosophy is on this topic.

Crucially, not all philosophies need be equally good. What makes a philosophy of *T* good? Here are some possibilities:

1. *Truth* is desirable in a philosophy. Presumably, some philosophies are wildly inaccurate, hence not insightful.

2. A philosophy of *T* could be more or less *deep*. Thinking harder about *T* might lead to reflecting on more fundamental aspects of *T*.

3. Some *topics* are deeper than others. All else being equal, a philosophy of people is deeper than a philosophy of cars or of cuisine.

4. A philosophy of *T* could be more, or it could be less, *rational*. It could rely upon more, or it could use less, good reasoning and evidence. In general, a more rational philosophy of *T* is preferable to a less rational one.

There are at least those ways for a given philosophy to be better or worse. Must a particular philosophy of *T* have one or more of these qualities if it is to be any good at all? A personal philosophy, for instance, no matter how sincerely believed, is not *thereby* good philosophy. Roughly, a good philosophy is genuinely explanatory – of something worth explaining. It is true, rational, and deep. And philosophy as a whole – as an 'official' discipline – is a vast number of people in various ways, both now and throughout history, individually and within groups, each seeking the best possible philosophy of one or more topics. Has anyone yet succeeded? Maybe. Can further philosophical progress still be made? Maybe.

So, let's think philosophically about reality and knowledge. Not only have these topics produced some of history's deepest and most sustainedly rational philosophies; many provocative questions remain unanswered; and thinking philosophically about such issues is a surprising way of *improving* as a person. It is not the only way to do so; nor can it ensure that welcome outcome. Used sensitively and carefully and sincerely, though, philosophical thinking can assist you in that process of self-improvement. Imagine coming to understand and care about such matters as truth, evidence, reason, fallibility, moral responsibility, the meanings of life and of death, and so on. In order to treat other people more fairly and considerately, say, it helps to be attuned to such aspects of your interactions with them: 'Where, in all of this, is real truth to be found? How is it most likely to be found? Could I have been mistaken? Am I responsible for what has occurred?' Philosophical richness is thus implicit even in everyday actions and interactions. Becoming more aware of it can deepen your understanding of those actions and interactions. It might enliven your mind with new possibilities for acting and interacting within the situation. Thinking philosophically about reality and knowledge could also broaden your sense of life's moral aspects. This is because part of maturing emotionally and intellectually *is* one's asking, answering, and applying to one's life, assorted questions that happen to be metaphysical and epistemological.

For example, it is immature to see oneself as always being correct; and doing so could involve one's philosophically misunderstanding the nature of truth. It is correlatively immature – and philosophically naive – to regard all of one's opinions as constituting knowledge or as being well supported by good evidence. Each of us needs at some time to begin trying to discern which ways of thinking do – and which do not – provide us with views that are true, rational, and knowledge. Not to make that attempt, while continuing to have views, is somewhat irresponsible. (And as you develop, shouldn't you confront more demanding standards of evidence and reasoning? Don't you need to meet higher standards than when you were a child?) Or are we adrift in a world we cannot comprehend, forming groundless opinions which we mistake for knowledge? It can be a touch scary to take such questions seriously. It can mean accepting that possibly we are deeply flawed in holding the views we do, perhaps that few, if any, of our beliefs are true or knowledge or supported by good evidence. But if you never confront such possibilities, you face the world as a correlatively less developed person. And epistemological thinking provides ways of confronting such possibilities consciously and conscientiously. As we mature, we should increasingly feel our fallibility, even while strengthening our real cognitive powers. How fallible are we? How do we nonetheless gain knowledge?

Metaphysical thinking is similarly important to growing emotionally and intellectually. To mature is, in part, to understand what one has in common with other people: you are whatever you are by having properties that others also share. Yet you remain a unique person too, different from others; and fundamentally, what does this involve? Might you have a singular capacity of thought or character, with which you can will or even partly control the nature of the world around you? Or are you always controlled instead? Is there a God watching over you and others? If not, can there be meaning to people's lives anyway? Why is death bad – if it is? Looking for philosophically good answers to questions like these can deepen and strengthen you as a person.

To think about metaphysics and epistemology, then, is to engage with many personally vital matters. And it is to think in ways that should contribute to one's maturing as a person – becoming an adult (in more than a merely biological sense), then becoming an increasingly thoughtful and insightful one. Philosophy has much potential to improve you as a person.

Using this Book

Themes Although this book is first and foremost about philosophies of reality and knowledge, it bears upon ethical and social values, too. For it indicates many ways in which thinking philosophically about reality and knowledge can suggest and deepen questions about right and wrong, good and evil. These links are rarely mentioned in metaphysics and epistemology textbooks. That is a pity. The existence of these connections gives us an added reason to *care* about metaphysics and epistemology.

I will introduce you to some of philosophy's most significant theories of reality and knowledge (both traditional theories and newer ones). Not every worthwhile thought that philosophers have had about reality and knowledge will be discussed; no short introduction could do that. Occasionally, I include an idea that might be original with me. But in general my aim is to explain other philosophers' thoughts, making clear why they deserve your attention. I do not agree with all of them; nor will you. Could they nevertheless be good philosophical thoughts – perhaps even true?

Questions Philosophical questions can be intellectually and emotionally liberating. However, they – and attempted answers to them – accomplish most when reflecting an understanding of existing ideas and theories. This book asks you many questions. Each extends some ideas that are explained in the book; yet each takes you beyond those theories – always intellectually, often emotionally. In particular, between each section and the next (within a given chapter), you will find a lengthy question. Most of these concern potential applications, to humanly significant issues, of some 'pure' metaphysics or epistemology from one or more of the surrounding sections. Each of these questions is suitable for use in class discussions. Many would be appropriate as essay questions. I have included questions that allow various ethical or 'political' leanings to be tested. (Some of those leanings will be mine; some will not.) I do this to stimulate, not to indoctrinate.

References   Each chapter concludes with a Further Readings section, where I list several books through which you can deepen your understanding of that chapter's topics. I list only books, because they are usually easier to find than are articles in specialist philosophy journals. Still, many important articles are subsequently reprinted in anthologies, and I do mention some of those. (For 'classic' works by famous deceased philosophers, I provide no publication details. These books have usually been published in various places.) I have not referred only to books with which I agree.

Attitudes   Eminent philosophers' theories often receive competing textual interpretations: '*P* was saying this' versus 'No, *P* was saying something else'. Nowhere in this book do I intend to be arguing for unusual or idiosyncratic interpretations of a given philosopher's theory. When explaining someone's ideas, my aim is to present a reasonably standard interpretation.

I also tend to avoid 'taking sides' on many of the issues being presented. But when I do express (and argue for) a philosophical preference, I know that I might be mistaken. Consequently, I accept the possibility of your being able to think of a better argument *against* the view I favour. So, by all means, if you suspect that I am wrong, seek the best evidence you can – by observing and thinking – to support your suspicion. And even if you believe that I am correct, try *testing* my view. Seek good evidence against it – before deciding whether, in the end, my view survives that test. Can you be both open-minded and critical? It is not easy. Yet it is important, both for doing philosophy well and for improving as a person. Good luck. Think hard. Observe carefully. And enjoy the effort.

Acknowledgments

I am grateful to the following people for their astute and thoughtful criticisms and questions, along with their support. Scott Campbell, Chuck Cross, Parveen Seehra, and Robert Young responded to the entire manuscript. Steve Buckle, Jim Franklin, Paula Gottlieb, and Tim Oakley read various sections or chapters. (Tom Baldwin's early advice on a section I decided not to write was useful, too.) And Jackie Jones's editorial guidance was valuable.

Persons

Physicalism

What are you – fundamentally? 'Fairly fundamentally, I am a person.' It would be rude to doubt the truth of that reply. But it could be philosophical without being at all rude to ask what makes you a person. Let's ask this about everyone, not only you. At first glance, it seems that we are *human beings*, members of a biological species. If so, then each of us is at least partly physical. Is that also all that we are? Many people find it natural to say that we are not merely physical – that there is some extra aspect to us, people being partly mental. (And there are those who are tempted to add: 'Other beings, unlike us, are merely physical. This makes us special.')

Yet that view of ourselves might be suspiciously self-flattering. I am not saying that it is false. We should think about whether it is, though, rather than simply assuming that it is true. So, here is a seemingly confronting hypothesis to ponder:

> You are just a moving, talking, lump of physical stuff.

This is a *physicalism* (or *materialism*, as philosophers also call it) about your metaphysical nature as a person. It implies that you are no less wholly physical than is a frog or a piece of gold. It implies that if a scientist could separate out every physical piece of you, no part or aspect of you would be left over.

'How could that be correct?' you might respond. 'My feelings and thoughts would be left over. My mind is real, even if it is not part of the physical world. I experience it, even if I do not see it.' A physicalist will probably reply to you in this way:

> You think and feel, only insofar as your physical bits are combined appropriately. Your thoughts and feelings are nothing above and beyond your body.

To put it bluntly: They are physical. Whatever is mental is also somehow physical. Your mental aspects are not made of non-physical stuff.

Imagine some neuroscientists closely observing your brain when you are feeling pain. Are they observing your feeling pain? Are they observing the pain itself? ('We see that you are feeling pain. And yes, we see your pain. It is in your brain ... *there*.') If physicalism is true, perhaps the scientists can indeed observe your being in pain without feeling it as you do. They would observe whatever physical aspect of you *is* the experience of pain.

But how would the scientists ever know that what they are observing is a feeling of pain? You might tell them that it is; do they know that you are telling the truth? How can they check on whether you are – without having some independent way of observing your pain? We will return to this issue in Chapter 12 (Other minds – where we encounter a challenge to our ever knowing of others' mental lives). Right now, though, we may simply raise the *possibility* that the neuroscientists, in observing whatever is physical about you, are not observing all that there is in you at that moment. Yet what else might there be?

Question 1.1 Is being a person inherently important or valuable? Is it vital to the world that there be people? (Is this a special world because it contains us?) Are you of value to the world, simply because you are a person (and irrespective of what you actually do)? Or must you earn whatever value you will ever have as a person? Do all people have an inherent moral significance beyond that, if any, which is possessed by other animals?

Immaterialism

That anti-physicalist suspicion at the end of the previous section often leads to this question:

Might it be that what is distinctive about being a person is something non-physical?

There is a tradition of thought that regards our ability to think – especially our apparent capacity to have thoughts about ourselves – as being what makes us persons. And maybe only people have real feelings, too. After all, as individual persons, we often think and feel that our uniqueness among persons in general is most vividly constituted by our particular thoughts and feelings. Even if someone else could look exactly like you, perhaps no one else thinks and feels exactly as you do.

So, many people accept *immaterialism*:

A person is non-physical.

For example, you are the specific person you are, by being identical with your non-physical thoughts and feelings. This is not to say that you lack a body. But might your body be an inessential part of you? Might it not be part of you, in some deeper and stricter sense? When you awake from sleep, even before your eyes open (allowing you to check that you have not metamorphosed into a fly overnight), are you already aware of yourself as being a person? The idea is that your body stands to your thoughts and feelings much as your clothes stand to your body. Your clothes 'house' your body. Might your body similarly 'house' your mind? (And just as your clothes do this temporarily, might your body be only a temporary home?) Perhaps your brain in particular 'houses' your mind. But much as your body can exist without clothes, then even if your thoughts are always accompanied by your having a brain, maybe the brain's presence is more a convenience than a necessity in your being a person – as clothes are a convenience, not a necessity.

How plausible is immaterialism? It does not clearly do justice to how we tend to think about personal harm and moral responsibility, for instance – vital phenomena in the experience and significance of being a person. To harm another's body is to harm the other person. If you punch someone, you injure a person, not only a body. This is so, even if the other person is unaware of being punched. (At the very least, you would have treated the other person as if he or she deserves no respect.) Nor can you escape being morally responsible for inflicting that harm, by pleading that it was not really you who harmed the other person's body. 'It wasn't me who injured him. Only my body did so.' If ever a plea sounds hollow, that one does.

Question 1.2   Could one human being be more a person than some other one is? (Or is being a person an absolute property?) For instance, does being more, rather than less, self-aware or morally sensitive or brave or empathetic make one literally more, rather than less, a person? Could someone's being more morally developed make them more a person? In general, is a child less a person than an adult is? Might a newly born child not even be a person? Do children need to develop morally, not just physically and psychologically, if they are to become people? Might substantial moral development be necessary for being – becoming – a person?

Dualism

Perhaps you seek a compromise between physicalism and immaterialism. Should we accept something along the following lines?

Each person is a blend of a physical body and a non-physical mind.

This hypothesis is usually called *dualism*. (Often it is termed *Cartesian* dualism, in honour of René Descartes. Later in this chapter, we see how he enters the story.) It conceives of each person as being a duality, combining two comparatively basic elements – a physical body and a non-physical mind. To many, this will sound basically correct: 'Of course I am both mind and body. Nothing could be more obvious.' Indeed, the success of some businesses is due to many people making dualistic assumptions about their underlying nature as persons. Festivals of Mind/Spirit and Body encourage us to bring our bodies 'into harmony with' our non-physical minds. (People often seem to think, too, that being at least partly non-physical makes us morally special beings. Is non-physical stuff morally superior to physical stuff?)

Nonetheless, dualism is not assumed by most philosophers to be true. Here is one puzzle about it. (This is called the 'causal interaction problem'. It is one vital aspect of *the mind-body problem*.) How could something non-physical be causally affected by something physical – and vice versa? If your mind is not physical, then your deciding to raise your arm is not part of the physical world. So, how could it operate causally as part of that world? Yet that is where your arm moves. If your mind does not operate there, where does the causation occur of which it is supposed to be a part? If the causal interaction is part of the physical world, so are whatever it links – in this case, your body and your mind. Alternatively, if the causal interaction is not part of the physical world, neither are whatever it links – in this case, your mind and your body. In either case, therefore, it is not clear how causal interaction can occur between a physical body and a non-physical mind. You could not raise your physical arm by deciding in your non-physical mind to do so. You would only *seem* to be having that effect via that means. The whole issue remains deeply perplexing. ('But if I gave up believing that part of me is non-physical, I would find the thought of my death overpowering.' This does not make that belief true, though. And should you find the prospect of death overpowering anyway? Maybe not; Chapter 5 will discuss that question.)

Question 1.3   Could a person forget how to be a person? If a human baby were to be 'adopted' by chimpanzees, would it become a person as it grew older among them? If a baby were to be imprisoned, alone, by his or her parents for thirteen years (as has in fact occurred), would he or she be a person once the imprisonment ended? If not, might he or she never become a person?

Questions of personal identity

Much contemporary philosophical discussion of the metaphysical nature of persons focuses on the nature of *personal identity*. This is one's being the same person over time – a single person over time. What makes you the same person today as you were yesterday? What makes you the same person today as you were fifteen years ago? If we do not know what makes you a single persisting person, perhaps we do not know what makes you a person at all, even at a specific time. Would something that is not a single person from one day to another fail ever to be a person?

These are difficult questions to answer, because there are many differences between you-fifteen-years-ago, you-yesterday, and you-today, say. There are differences in what you look like, sound like, and so on; there are differences in what thoughts and feelings you have. So, *is* there in fact a single you, persisting over those fifteen years? That is, does *numerical* identity – a single person – persist throughout those qualitative changes? If it does, there can be numerical identity even when qualitative identity is absent. Yet if you-at-a-given-time are just a blend of various features, and if at each time a new blend exists, then where – literally where – is there a continuing you, persisting over time? Perhaps nothing is shared by those disparate blends; in which case, possibly there is no you – no 'overall you'. And insofar as we are uncertain about that, we might also have doubts as to whether there is even a real you right now. For we might wonder what it takes to be a single person even at a single time – given that we would have expected such a person to be numerically identical to various people existing at other times.

Question 1.4 We talk of some actions as being inhuman. Is someone who acts in such a way literally not being a person at that time? (Is he or she being an anti-person?) Is it possible to be a person at some times and not at others? Are murderers or torturers not persons when performing those vile actions? Would they appear to be persons – by looking like they are – without really being persons at such moments? If they have too many such moments, do they cease being persons at all in their lives? ('But if one is not a person when acting so badly, should we not hold anyone morally or legally responsible for such actions? That is an intolerable thought.' Indeed it is. Can we hold a person responsible, though, for having acted unlike a person? Or should we cease thinking of people as being so good that evil actions are called inhuman?)

'No longer the same person'

There is an everyday way of talking which encourages the dire thought at the end of the previous section. Suppose that you say, for example, 'I have changed so much that I am no longer the same person as I was five years ago.' Could you mean that literally? Five years ago there was a person with a bunch B of properties; today there is a person with a bunch B^* of properties; and, insofar as 'you have changed so much', B^* is very different from B. (For instance, the B-person was a sexually promiscuous alcoholic, whereas the B^*-person is teetotal and faithfully married.) If the B-person was you, and if the B^*-person is so different from the B-person as to be a different person, then you no longer exist. Conversely, if the B^*-person is you, and if the B^*-person is so different from the B-person as to be a different person, then you did not exist five years ago.

Nor need you have had recent significant experiences (such as giving up alcohol and becoming married) in order for that conceptual challenge to arise. Let C be a collection of some child's properties (in fact, those which you regard as having been yours at an early stage of your life); C is very different from A, an agglomeration of some adult's properties (in fact, those which you regard as being yours now). If the C-person was you, and if the existence of a significant qualitative difference between two bundles of properties prevents there being just one person present, then you never became an adult: you would not now exist. Conversely, if the A-person is you, and if the existence of a significant qualitative difference between two bundles of properties prevents there being just one person present, then you never were a child: you would never have existed back then. Such reasoning arises for any adult and any child. It gives us this general result:

> No child is the same person as some adult which he or she seems to have become.

And few of us will feel comforted by that thought, to say the least.

Question 1.5   Are conjoined twins always clearly two people (as you and your best friend are clearly two people)? Or might they be a single person – by being an interestingly complex and different kind of person? If they were to think of themselves as being just one person, would this be enough to make them one person?

Conventionalism

The last section's remarkable reasoning depends upon interpreting as being literal a widespread way of talking which describes someone as having changed so much as no longer to be the same person as before. 'Then don't interpret that way of talking literally,' you might say, 'It is merely loose and suggestive – like all talk of personal identity.'

What surprising thinking might prompt that last claim? Here is one candidate, a *conventionalist* one:

> There is no real and definite fact as to whether you-today are the same person as you-yesterday, beyond whether we are willing to *call* the two of you the one

overall you. There is nothing more to your being a person than a word such as 'person' being applied to you, or than others thinking of you as being one. Being a person is simply a social convention.

But how could that be correct? Suppose that people had never thought of words for themselves (such as the word 'person'). Then we would never describe ourselves as being people. Yet we would still *be* people. If so, then being called a person is not what makes you a person.

So, there might also be a moral danger in conventionalism about the metaphysical nature of persons. Consider those people who were slaves in America (or, for that matter, the many people who are slaves even now around the world). Surely they were people even when deemed legally not to be. Other people – including all or most of those with legal power in that context – denied that the term 'person' applied to slaves. However, now we think that those denials were incorrect – not only morally unfortunate, but metaphysically incorrect. The slaves were people in virtue of their own properties, irrespective of what others named them. That is, they were intrinsically persons. Being a person does not await a decision by others. Although a linguistic community can decide what words to use in describing a person, those speakers are not making the person a person (by calling him or her a person) or turning the person into something other than a person (by denying that he or she is a person). Even a law that calls slaves non-persons would not make them non-persons. Legally, it would do so (within a given legislative domain); metaphysically, it would not. Being a person is an aspect of reality we do not create simply by deciding to speak in a particular way.

Question 1.6   Would any legislation – such as was proposed in America in 2001 (by the president and Republican members of Congress) – decreeing that a fertilised human egg is to be a person fail to bring about that metaphysical outcome? Would such a law be merely political or ideological? Could it be metaphysically *mistaken* as to what a person is? Should that possibility worry the legislation's proponents?

Descartes on what persons are

Perhaps the most famous philosophical attempt to understand what it is to be a person was made by the French philosopher René Descartes (1596–1650), particularly in his *Meditations on First Philosophy* (1641). His *Meditations* are especially notable for three ideas. In 'Meditation I' Descartes asks, strikingly, what he knows (and in Chapters 11 and 12 we will see how he motivated that question). In 'Meditation II' he claims to know that he is immaterial; in 'Meditation VI' his immaterialism is replaced by his dualism. Let's briefly consider his immaterialism.

When Descartes reflects (in 'Meditation I') on what he can know with certainty, at first he decides that nothing passes this test: doubts, even when unlikely, remain possible. Then he reasons that there is some knowledge which no doubts can unsettle. His reasoning was along these lines:

> Even when trying to doubt everything, I know that I am doubting! And I know that doubting is a way of thinking. I also know that even if my other thoughts – those whose truth I am doubting – are false, I am still *thinking* them. One way or another, then, I can know that I am thinking.

What else does this tell Descartes? If he knows that he is thinking, he also knows that he *exists*; or so he infers. In his *Discourse on Method* (1637) he summed up this inference, in French, with 'I think, therefore I am'. Later (not in the *Meditations*), this was translated into Latin, as *Cogito ergo sum* – which is why this aphorism is generally called the *Cogito*. It is one of philosophy's most famous thoughts. It is Descartes's being unable to doubt his own existence, even while accepting that he can doubt the accuracy of such beliefs as those about his body – including his having one! It is Descartes's inferring from this that he – whom he knows to exist while thinking – is something distinct from his body – which he does not know to exist. It is Descartes's knowing himself only as a thinking thing, not a bodily thing. (Indeed, it is his knowing himself as a thinker only when he is thinking: he knows only of his actively thinking.)

Here are two of the many questions that philosophers have raised about this reasoning by Descartes.

1. Is it possible to have a body *inessentially*? In Chapter 6 (Essentialism), we will ask whether something can have both essential and inessential properties. Even if your mind is the more entrenched part of you, might your body still be part – albeit an inessential part – of you?

2. Is it possible that knowledge need not be as demanding as Descartes assumes? In particular, can you know, with something *less* than certainty or infallibility, what you are? Might you know of the presence of both your body and your mind – while nonetheless knowing of your body somewhat less securely than you know of your mind? Chapters 9 and 12 discuss the nature of knowledge in detail (and they will explain the idea of less demanding knowledge).

Question 1.7   Do those who become amnesiacs cease to be persons? Have they at least stopped being the persons they were (becoming numerically new persons)? Or do they become what we might call partial persons, lacking something that is required for being fully a person? (Is there any sense in which each of us is only a partial person?) Now apply these questions anew, to those suffering from Alzheimer's disease. Does that dire disease strip them of, literally, their identities? Do differences wrought in them by the disease prevent their being – literally – the persons they previously were? In each case, has one person ceased to exist, a second one taking their place in the world? (Or would you continue caring about your Alzheimer's-afflicted parent, say, because his or her *body* is still alive? Is a persisting body therefore a persisting person?)

Locke on personal identity

I began this chapter by asking whether persons are simply human beings – biological beings. That question was also posed in the seventeenth century, by the English philosopher John Locke (1632–1704). His controversial analysis of personal identity distinguished a person's identity over time from a human being's (or a man's, to use his term). For Locke, a human being is a functioning animal body – whereas without a continuing stream of consciousness of oneself, there is no single ongoing person (no matter how much one looks like a single person living a sustained life during that time). Locke would say that you-today are the same person as you-yesterday only if you-today have a sense of yourself that includes a memory of yourself-yesterday. (For example, you recall some of what you thought and felt yesterday.) But what of you-today and you-fifteen-years-ago, say? Quite possibly, you-today and you-fifteen-years-ago fail Locke's criterion. (It would be a singular achievement to remember one's exploits on every previous day of one's life, or even on an arbitrary day fifteen years ago. And sometimes we try to forget what we have done or suffered.) If so, then Locke's analysis would entail that you-the-overall-person did not exist fifteen years ago, as you-fifteen-years-ago.

Locke would not be perturbed by that implication. He might agree that you-the-one-human-being have existed for those fifteen years, without conceding that there has been a single you-the-person existing for all of that time. The one body could have contained different persons over those years, he would think. Indeed, Locke would not have ended his surprising speculations there. He even allows that in theory a single person could occupy different bodies over time – and that in theory a single person could occupy different parts of a body over time! Locke imagines someone's consciousness accompanying their little finger – yes, their little finger – when it becomes separated from the rest of their body. The little finger would be the bodily 'home' of that stage of that person.

Why was Locke so willing to accept that apparently bizarre implication of his theory? Why did he think that we should distinguish between human beings and persons? His suggestion's significance is intended to be partly moral: When blame or praise are appropriate, who should receive it? A human being? A person? If you retain no consciousness of having defrauded others, is punishment of the human-being-that-is-your-body not really punishment of the person who acted badly? For Locke, that is indeed so. Yet in practice we do generally punish the living body; we assume that it is the person. If Locke is right, we might sometimes be mistaken. Mostly, the same human being generally is the same Lockean person, at least over short periods of time. But Locke says that the human being who is punished might not ultimately – from God's perspective – be the correct person to be punished. We do the best we can, with our more limited perspectives, in judging such matters. Is that good enough, metaphysically speaking? Should our practices of praise and blame continue to be applied to human beings, irrespective of whether they are Lockean persons? Which is the more fundamental category – human being? person?

Question 1.8   Are there emotions that only a person can have? ('Love!' But might apes and elephants, for a start, also feel this?) Are there emotions that a person – in order to be a person – must feel sometimes, or at least feel in appropriate circumstances? In dehumanising Jews as they did, explicitly degrading Jews, treating them as non-persons, did Nazis unwittingly lose their own humanity – 'shutting down', or never feeling, many important emotions within themselves? Did they cease being persons – without realising it?

Hume on personal identity

You might remain confident that there is a special, simple way in which you know of your personal identity over time. You might say that you can directly experience – by being introspectively aware of – a Single Self, an Internal 'I', a Separate Substance Within, perhaps a Cartesian immaterial substance: 'When I am aware of myself, I am aware of my own self. It is what persists within me – *as* me, strictly speaking. Even when I have new thoughts or experiences, there must be a continuing Me having them.'

However, is it so obvious that there is a continuing Internal You? That question was advanced memorably by the Scottish philosopher David Hume (1711–76). He wanted to know whether anyone experiences themselves as a persisting internal personal substance. It is trivial for you to claim to be aware of yourself as an ongoing internal self. But are you ever genuinely aware of such an entity? Pause for a moment;

try to be literally Self-aware; catch your Self 'in the act' of having experiences. You can be aware of the experiences themselves: you are aware of one thought, now of another; you experience a particular emotion, then a new one; you enjoy a memory, followed by a further one; and so on. Is there also a further awareness, of the self as such, the 'I' – *apart from* the awarenesses of those thoughts and feelings? Trying to find it will just make you aware of another *experience* – another thought or emotion or memory, say. The question remains of how you could know that this new experience belongs to the same internal self as do the others. For example, how could Descartes know that an I-now, experienced at one moment of thinking, is the same I as an I-now who is experienced at another moment of thinking?

Hume proposed an answer to this sort of puzzle. He did not argue that there are no selves – that there is no you. Instead, he urged us to revise our conception of what a self is. On Hume's conception, each self is simply a collection of internal, mental, experiences. A self is not something extra, separate from its experiences. Hume thought that all talk of oneself as a special and separate self was a mere fiction, a simplifying convenience. Rather (in his view), the self is literally a bundle of internal experiences. By definition, even slightly different experiences would constitute a different bundle – and thereby a literally, numerically, new person. You are simply your thoughts and feelings. Although it could be comforting to think that there is something more to you – an underlying, persisting, extra self – what is comforting need not be true.

Yet that comforting thought is also part of how many people seek to understand themselves as being metaphysically special beings. They might muse as follows, for instance:

> My unique and separate self is autonomous, exercising a free will. It is an engine of reason, too, fundamentally a home of knowledge. Perhaps it has a spiritual aspect, due in part to there being a God. And it binds my life's experiences into a meaningful whole. It could even survive bodily death. (What is more, it has these various properties essentially.)

That beguiling thinking paints what many people hope is an accurate self-portrait.

However, we should not *assume* that we are or have selves with those noteworthy properties. Only our deepest and best reflection can justify any confidence that we have them. So, we must reach for philosophy, because assessing whether we have such properties is a key philosophical project. Beginning in the next chapter, then, much of this book asks whether we are indeed special in those ways.

Question 1.9 Suppose that Hume is right to deny that people are constituted, even in part, by a separate and united self. Should this change how you treat other people? Does it justify treating them badly? Or if a person just is a bundle of experiences, is it especially important to *improve* the quality of other people's experiences? (After all, if that is what a person is, would this be the only way to respect and to help another person?) Could you be improving the people themselves, by assisting their having pleasurable and worthwhile experiences?

Singer on non-human persons

The first section began with a seemingly innocent assumption – namely, that all persons are human beings. Since then, we have confronted this question: What else (if anything) is needed if a human being is to be a person? But the controversial Australian philosopher Peter Singer (b. 1946) has questioned that initial assumption. He denies that all persons are human beings. Of course, insofar as human beings are physical beings, immaterialists likewise deny that all people are human beings (because they deny that people are ever human beings). Singer is not an immaterialist, though: he is not saying that no persons are human beings. Instead, his thesis is that only some persons are human beings. You are a human being, as am I. Which people are not? Look around you; where are they?

You might be surprised. Singer first became famous for his philosophical defence of what he called animal liberation. He regards it as *speciesism* (a word akin to 'racism' and 'sexism') never to accord other animals genuine moral standing. If an animal can feel pain, it is thereby like human beings in a morally vital respect. But some animals are also like us in respects which, we might believe, *make* us persons. Singer argues that if those animals have the same features that suffice for our being persons, then those animals, too, are persons. And are there any such animals? Indeed there are (says Singer): apes are persons. Locke (in the section, Locke on personal identity) thought that the capacity to be aware of oneself existing over time makes one a person; and there is good evidence of apes having that same capacity. We feel emotions and we reason; so, it seems, do apes. Accordingly (concludes Singer), we should classify apes as persons. (Perhaps we should regard some other animals, such as dolphins and elephants, similarly. Our relevant evidence regarding apes is stronger right now.)

Singer's conclusion is provocative; is it nonetheless true? And does it imply, for instance, that human beings and apes always have the *same* moral status? Even if apes are persons, whenever their interests clash with those of human beings are ours more morally important?

Further reading

On personal identity in general:

Brian Garrett, *Personal Identity and Self-Consciousness* (London: Routledge, 1998).

Jonathan Glover, *I: The Philosophy and Psychology of Personal Identity* (London: Penguin, 1988).

Jeff McMahan, *The Ethics of Killing: Problems at the Margins of Life* (New York: Oxford University Press, 2002), ch. 1.

Derek Parfit, *Reasons and Persons* (Oxford: Clarendon Press, 1984), chs 10, 11.

John Perry, *A Dialogue on Personal Identity and Immortality* (Indianapolis: Hackett, 1978).

For Descartes on persons:

René Descartes, *Meditations on First Philosophy*, I, II, and VI.

For Locke on personal identity:

John Locke, *An Essay Concerning Human Understanding*, Bk II, ch. XXVII.

For Hume on personal identity:

David Hume, *A Treatise of Human Nature*, Bk I, Part IV, sec. VI.

For Singer on non-human persons:

Peter Singer, *Rethinking Life and Death: The Collapse of our Traditional Ethics* (New York: St Martin's Press, 1994), ch. 8.

2

Free Will

Determinism

Imagine a rock crashing through your window. What else must that story include? Given how the physical world is, once the rock was oh-so-close, the window had no chance of surviving intact: its shattering was caused by the rock's impact. So, at some stage in the world's history, the window's breaking became inevitable. Was that so, only when the rock's arrival was imminent? Or, even one hundred years earlier, say, was the world already proceeding inexorably towards your window's being smashed by that rock? *Somewhere* in the past, enough had occurred to bring about your window's demise.

At any rate, that is how a *causal determinist* interprets the situation. Unrestricted causal determinism is this thesis:

> For anything that occurs, something in the past made it occur.

In other words, whatever occurs was caused to occur. This is more than its occurrence being made probable by what the world was already like. Whatever occurs does so because something else has occurred or been 'in place' – something which *suffices* for bringing it about, thereby guaranteeing its occurring.

But wait a moment: among the things that occur are your thoughts and actions. Does determinism purport to apply to them, too? Certainly an unrestricted determinism does – by implying this:

> For any thought or action of yours, something in the past made it occur.

Any thought you have, any action you perform, is rendered inescapable – given some prior state of the world. Your reading this book, your scratching your head, and so on – determinism insists that something had already occurred or been 'in place', somewhere in the past, which sufficed for your performing these actions. It is not merely that your actions have been *influenced* by the past. It is that, given some prior aspect of the world, you *could not* have acted differently. Your opportunities for alternative thoughts and actions would be nonexistent. Causally, the past suffices for – and thereby makes – the future; or so say determinists.

Question 2.1   Have your political views, or your religious ideas, or your beliefs about morality been forced upon you by aspects of your past? (How would you know that this has not occurred?) Indeed, the same question arises for all of your views. Or can you always – freely, afresh – change your mind? And if you can always do that, then how deeply or committedly do you ever believe? Are your beliefs only shallowly held? (How can you know that they are not?)

Fatalism

Determinism should be distinguished from fatalism. Whereas determinism tells us that aspects of the past have rigorously and fully caused whatever has subsequently happened, fatalism does not depend on claims about how the world is causally structured. Whereas determinism's full name is 'causal determinism', fatalism could be called 'metaphysical', or perhaps 'logical', fatalism – deriving its dramatic claims via abstract reasoning about truth and reality. Fatalism says that whatever happens does so as part of the entire history of this world, with no change to that history ever having been possible. Any such change is impossible because this world as a whole comprises whatever is, whatever has been, and whatever will be. That entirety *is* this world. And it is *already* this world – including, right now, its having whatever future it will have. Whatever happens in our world is essential to it. (In Chapter 6 (Essentialism) I will outline more fully what it is to have a particular property essentially.)

Accordingly, a fatalist might argue along the following lines. Suppose that it will be true in five minutes' time that a rock is then breaking your window. In that event, it is true now that in five minutes' time a rock will be breaking your window. By the same token, though, it was true one hundred years ago that in five minutes' time from now a rock will be breaking your window. Indeed, it was always true, at any time in the past, that in five minutes' time from now a rock will be breaking your window. Hence, there is nothing you could have done to prevent that fate for your window. Even one hundred years ago, the window's fate had been decided – long before that window had been thought of, let alone come into existence.

And fatalists reason like that about *all* facts. Fatalism requires just the idea that if (for example) you are scratching your head right now, it is true at any other time – including any time in the past – that at this time you are scratching your head. Whatever is was always going to be – because it is. Whatever will be was always going to be – because it will be.

Will fatalism therefore encourage some disturbing attitudes? Does it imply that we should stop caring about the future, striving to bring about one future rather than another? Would there be no point in deliberating as to whether to help someone in distress? ('Why should I bother? If they're to be saved, it's already true that they will be saved. I can't change that. Nor can I change it if they aren't to be saved'.) Determinism, too, is sometimes thought to generate fatalist attitudes: 'If everything is causally determined, then the causal pattern has already begun which will, or will not, result in the person's being saved. It's too late for me to decide whether to help.'

But perhaps those attitudes arise through misunderstanding fatalism. If fatalism is true, there is a future which you cannot prevent occurring; nonetheless, its occurring could depend on how you act right now – which might even involve your having deliberated before acting. And we can still try to act morally, because there continue to be morally better or worse outcomes. Your acting in some particular way now might be exactly what is needed if someone's pain and suffering is to be eased tomorrow, for instance. Trying to act well might be a necessary prelude to acting well; perhaps *all* of this is unavoidable for you. Your trying to act well – after wondering whether to do so – could have already been destined to occur! Fatalism is no foe of our trying to act well.

Question 2.2 'Nature – our genes – makes us what we are.' 'No, nurture – family, society – does so.' 'You are both wrong. It's a combination of the two.' Do these three claims exhaust the relevant possibilities? If so, is everything about you causally determined in one of these ways? Or could you be what you are, at a given time, without having been caused to be so?

What is free will?

Many people feel threatened when alerted to the possibility that either determinism or fatalism is true. Accordingly, it is not unusual to encounter vehement denials that either of those doctrines is true – or at least that either is true of us, even if they happen to be true of much else in the world. ('We are free in many of our thoughts and actions. Maybe slugs aren't, though.') Yet if neither determinism nor fatalism is true of us, what does this reveal about how we think and act? If these doctrines leave us untouched, which competing doctrine explains why and how we do whatever we do? The most popular answer is that there is something special about people: We have *free wills*, with many of our thoughts and actions being free.

People often become passionate about this. Why should it matter so much to so many to believe that we have free wills? We observe what we take to be people performing what we take to be actions with which they can identify; apparently, we care that we are thereby observing people manifesting a capacity for metaphysical freedom. It cannot be that acting on this basis guarantees people good fortune in their lives. After all, it would be possible for us, even if we have free wills, to live miserably. Equally, it would be possible, even when living a causally determined life, to enjoy great accomplishment, goodness, and pleasure. What is so desirable or important, then, about having a free will? *Should* we regard free will so highly, becoming agitated at the determinist's or fatalist's claim that we lack it? The sections, Moral responsibility and Hume's compatibilism, focus on this question; let's first (in this section and the next two) become clearer on what free will is.

Suppose that Dave insults you, brazenly, unprovokedly. Do you have a choice as to how to respond? Could you ignore him? Can you insult him in return? You will in fact respond in one of these ways. And standard philosophical analysis tells us that, so long as it was possible for you to perform either action, whichever one you do perform is done freely.

Suppose, however, that there is great social pressure upon you, making it impossible in practice for you to ignore Dave (even though in theory you could either ignore him or insult him). Maybe within your social setting insults are meant to be met with insults; maybe in practice you are incapable of not conforming to that custom. Possibly, although you want to ignore Dave, you could not live with the social disgrace of not insulting him in return. The result is the socially acceptable one: You insult him! Given those social pressures, therefore, is your action not actually free? Is your will – your capacity to intend and decide – not free in this social setting? (The action of ignoring Dave was possible in itself for you – although not so, given the social pressures.)

This is a realistic case. People often plead social pressures as a reason – indeed, as an excuse – for their performing unfortunate or unsavoury actions: 'I couldn't help it. Everyone else was doing it, too.' And philosophers differ over how to analyse such cases. Here is one way of doing so:

> People *can* resist social pressures – performing, on occasions, morally good deeds disapproved of by other people around them. If you insult Dave because you cannot withstand various social pressures, your will in that setting is not free. If this happens repeatedly, to this extent your will in general is not free!

To which you might reply:

> My will remains free. If it is 'restricted' only by my *valuing* others' approval of
> what I do, then it is not really restricted. In doing what I value, I act as I want
> to act. That is freedom.

But might your own values render you unfree? If you cannot change
them, are you trapped by them? How deeply free must you be (in your
values, your desires, and so on), if your will is to be free?

Question 2.3   When an animal raised in captivity is released, it can flounder,
unable to fend for itself. If children are prematurely 'set free', abandoned, they can
flounder, unable to fend for themselves. Is valuable freedom somewhat capable
freedom? And is it learned, not innate? Must a capacity for real and worthwhile
freedom be developed over time – gained carefully, perhaps even with assistance
from others? Is valuable freedom somewhat controlled – limited – freedom?

Indeterminism

So far, we have highlighted only part of what it might take to be acting
freely. If you are responding freely to Dave, this is not simply, if at all,
because you could have responded differently from how you are
responding. What else is needed? Suppose that although it is possible
for you to ignore Dave and possible for you to insult him, over neither
of these ways of acting do you have any deliberate *control*. You can try
to do so – but, really, each will 'just occur'. You could watch your body
do whatever it does in response to Dave. You might feel in control of it.
But in fact you are not controlling or guiding your reaction. (You are
'reading, not writing', this page in the book of your life.) Consequently
(many philosophers will infer), in that circumstance you would not
clearly be acting freely in the sense of controlledly and deliberately
putting into effect a preference of yours.

Yet your response would not be causally determined, either. By
hypothesis, it was possible for you to have responded differently –
whereas causal determinism allows you no such latitude. So, although
your response to Dave is not causally determined, we have seen just now
why it might fall short of being an expression of free will. What more is
needed for metaphysical freedom?

If you are not controlling or guiding your response to Dave, maybe
it is too *random* to be free. You could have ignored him; alternatively,
you could have insulted him (as in fact you did); but the existence of
these two possibilities might be due merely to randomness. And would
such randomness place you 'at a distance from' your response? Would
it fundamentally not be *you* ignoring or insulting Dave, due to your not

controlling your doing so? Perchance, you would never know what you are going to do – only ever knowing instead what you have *done*. In short, is your action's not being causally determined compatible with your still not autonomously guiding that action? An absence of causal determinism seems to open up the possibility of an underlying randomness pervading the situation.

That is because the absence of determinism could simply be the presence of *indeterminism* – this denial of causal determinism:

> Some occurrences were not made – caused – to occur.

And wherever indeterminism applies (some philosophers have argued), there is no free will. Indeterminism allows actions to be performed, for instance, which no one really controls. An action or thought produced indeterministically is one for which no prior aspect of the world is enough to bring it about. Such actions 'just occur', with the past providing no full causal explanation of their doing so. If causal determinism's applying to you is like your being a puppet, controlled by a puppeteer, then indeterminism's applying to you leaves open the possibility of your being a puppet, still controlled – but now, paradoxically, by an unpredictable, *out*-of-control, puppeteer. (And I write this as the son of a puppeteer.) If that is what your actions are like, they are not clearly manifestations of a free will worth wanting – a will which can be part of a full causal explanation provided by the past of your acting as you do.

Accordingly, why can indeterminism – one's not being causally determined – initially sound so appealing? ('I really hope that I'm not a causally determined creature!') Is it because we assume that indeterminism would apply to us in a *desirable* way – by making available to our stable mind and body alternative possible ways of acting and thinking, between which we would then choose controlledly? But that assumption need not be true. Maybe indeterminism would apply to us in an unwelcome way. It might not allow our mind and body to be stable in the first place. Nor need it permit us the power of choosing controlledly (even if it allows us to feel like we have that power). There is a danger that, if you are not causally determined, your actions will feel free only because you cannot control or direct your mind sufficiently to *notice* the indeterministic randomness in your thinking and acting.

Question 2.4 Some people say that part of the appeal in becoming drunk is the possibility of 'losing control'. Why would that be appealing? Might one's having such control be a necessary component in being a person? Some people say that, when drunk, they become more free in how they act. Yet isn't it usually all-too-predictable how a drunk person will act? (Maybe, even if uninhibited, they are too undisciplined to be fundamentally and interestingly free.) Could being drunk be a way (perhaps unintentionally) of allowing something else to control one's thoughts and actions? If so, would any accompanying feelings of freedom be illusory?

Evidence of free will?

Few people concede that indeterminism governs their thoughts and actions. Most of us think that we have extremely good evidence of our having a free will. That evidence is of various happenings within us. Often, we act on the bases of thinking about alternative actions, having preferences as to possible outcomes, and making decisions as to what to do. And so many people are sure that everyone has a free will, if only because each person can think and choose and decide and form preferences. Is everyone free in at least this way? (If you think so, you might also believe that there is a Special Enduring You, guiding your thoughts and actions, knowable only by you. Recall Hume's criticism of this idea, though, in Chapter 1 (Hume on personal identity).)

Yet could your feeling sure that you are choosing, thinking for yourself, considering alternative possible actions, or simply having preferences of your own, be misleading? Might your feeling of having a free will be causally determined itself? Could it be an inaccurate feeling which makes you feel better about yourself? For example, if your mind is wholly physical (a possibility discussed in Chapter 1 (Physicalism)), and if everything physical is caused in accord with the laws of nature by what has already occurred or been 'in place', then even your decisions and choices are causally determined. And even if your mind is not wholly physical (because either immaterialism or dualism is true, options considered in Chapter 1 (Immaterialism, Dualism)), could there nonetheless be patterns of thought which these not-wholly-physical minds routinely follow in various situations, reacting to what has already occurred or been 'in place'? Even if minds are not wholly physical, they might still be predictable in how they function. We might be less creative or original, significantly less in control of our thoughts, than we like to believe we are.

Our evidence for our having free wills is therefore inconclusive. This does not entail that we lack free wills, but it does raise that possibility. Would it really be disastrous, however, if we were to lack free will? We would believe ourselves to be deciding and choosing freely, and often to be acting on the basis of our freely deciding and choosing. Yet this belief would be false – no matter that we would not feel its falsity. Would its falsity imply anything regrettable or unsatisfactory or disturbing about us?

Would it make us non-persons, for instance? You might – or might not – think that having a free will is essential to being a person. Still, does being a person require at least that one seems to oneself to have a free will? (Do you think that a slug feels that it has a free will? Will an ostrich do so? What of a lion?) When people are brainwashed, all or some of their abilities to choose and decide for themselves disappear. They might even realise this, granting to some other person or organisation the right to choose and decide for them. Would this take away part of their personhood? Are they lessened – literally – as persons in that circumstance? What if they willingly choose to be unable forevermore to choose for themselves?

Question 2.5   Many cult leaders know how to brainwash and control people. Are there other – more widely respected – aspects of society that do likewise? Is it possible to be controlled so as to act uncontrolledly – randomly? Is there an inherent value in not being controlled by others? Is there an inherent value in having self-control? Is a capacity for self-control 'given' to us? Is a complete lack of it incompatible with being a person? Is a substantial amount of it needed if one is to be a person?

Moral responsibility

There is a further reason why many people feel threatened by the possibility of causal determinism. If our thoughts and actions are causally determined, the world's past leaves us no options beyond thinking and acting as we do. And we might wonder whether this would make it always false or meaningless to say that someone has thought or acted *morally* or *immorally*. You have acted morally or immorally, let's suppose, if the action in question has a moral dimension and it is an action for which you are morally responsible. Yet how can you be morally responsible for insulting Dave, say, if the past left you unable not to perform that action? Could you rightly be praised or blamed for your action, if the world's history gave you no possibility of not doing it? ('It's not my fault. With my past, how could I not have done that?') Many people, it seems, accept that if causal determinism obtains, then no one is morally responsible for his or her actions – because causal determinism 'forces' our actions upon us. We might therefore wonder whether, if causal determinism obtains, none of our actions are moral or immoral.

Perhaps causal determinism is not that dangerous, though. Suppose that you give money to Amnesty International, money which will ultimately contribute to saving some innocent person's life. Suppose that you do this because, being that kind of person, you experienced an overpowering urge to make that contribution. Are you morally responsible for your contributing the money, even though your caring character left you unable not to do so? Presumably, we may praise your morally good action, in spite of its being an inevitable consequence of your nature and circumstances. Analogously, may we still morally condemn people who treat others cruelly, for instance, even when their doing so flows inevitably from their natures and circumstances?

The most notable argument for that proposed compatibility of causal determinism with moral responsibility comes from the American philosopher Harry Frankfurt (b. 1929). He argued by describing a sort of circumstance (now generally called a *Frankfurt-style case*) in which, he claimed, someone is morally responsible for an action in spite of having been unable not to perform it. If such circumstances are possible, then even causal determinism's leaving you unable to act other than you do need not prevent your being morally responsible for at least some of your actions. For example, you want and intend to punch Dave; you plan your attack carefully – and successfully. (The deed is done.) Suppose, though, that a computer chip had been implanted in your brain without your realising it. And suppose that this allowed Dave's childhood enemy, Evad, not only to monitor your thinking, but to have *made* you punch Dave if you had been about to change your mind. (You would not have noticed being made to do so.) Hence, unwittingly, you cannot have avoided hitting Dave: although you think that you could have avoided doing so, you are mistaken! Do you nonetheless remain morally responsible for your punching him? Frankfurt would say so. Is your being morally responsible for an action thus not ruled out even if you were unable to act differently?

Question 2.6 Are you morally responsible for your character? 'I am morally responsible for some of it, as it continues to develop, partly under my control.' 'Is that clearly true? You can improve only what is already there, using what is already there – and you did not create any of that.' Are 'self-help' books incorrect when implying, as some seem to do, that you can wholly create and control your character? Can you be morally responsible for what you do, in spite of not having created what you are?

Foreknowledge

Throughout philosophy's history, the belief that people have free will has been challenged not only by the possibilities of causal determinism, fatalism, and indeterminism. The possibility of *foreknowledge*, too, has sometimes been thought to be incompatible with our having free will.

Usually, God's foreknowledge in particular is discussed, along the following lines:

> Suppose that there is an omniscient God – who therefore knows all that has happened, all that is happening, all that will happen. God knows, even before you have a particular thought or perform a particular action, what you are going to think or do. Consequently, you could not have thought or acted differently; otherwise, God would have known of this alternative future thought or action instead. (For knowledge is always of what is actual or true, as Chapter 9 (A traditional conception of knowledge) will explain.) So, if there is an omniscient God, you have no free will – insofar as you are never able to think or act differently from how in fact you think or act.

Those many people who doubt that there is an omniscient God anyway need not find that particular argument worrying. However, can it be extended so as to apply to all foreknowledge, thereby becoming more challenging? Is our having free will threatened even by the prospect of people having ordinary foreknowledge (rather than just God's doing so)? By adapting the previous paragraph's reasoning accordingly, we would derive this more general challenge:

> Whenever it is possible for someone to know in advance what another person will think or do in a specific situation, the latter person is 'trapped' in that respect. If I understand you well enough to know how you will react to seeing some upsetting incident, then you will react as I predict. Once I have that knowledge, you are unable to act differently from how I predict.

'No, of course I can act differently,' you might reply. But you are therefore *denying* that someone could ever understand you well enough to know, in advance, what you will do on some occasion. Be aware, however, that the argument is not depending on the clearly contentious claim that someone could ever know, in advance, *and with certainty*, what you will do. The argument says only that if someone could know in advance what you will do, then – because knowledge is of what is true – it is already true on that occasion that you will act as that person thinks you will act. And even if no one could know this with certainty, could they know it in some weaker and more everyday way? We often do talk as if one person can know what another is about to do. Perhaps your thinking that you can act differently is only your not knowing what you will do. Yet no one is so unformed by his or her past or nature or circumstances as never to think or act somewhat predictably. This might enable others to know what a person is going to do, at least sometimes. ('But it is impossible ever to know what is *going* to occur.' Chapter 12 (Hume on induction) presents that worry. 'Such knowledge would be impossible because knowledge is always based on certainty, something we lack in thinking about the future.' Maybe knowledge does *not* always require certainty, though – as Chapter 9 and Chapter 12 (Knowing fallibly, Improved knowledge) will explain.)

Question 2.7   Might only some of us have free wills? Are there ways to help a person's will to become more free? Are there ways in which a person's will could become less free – for example, if his or her body is severely restricted for a long time, or if his or her will is not used often enough? ('Use it – or lose it.') Can a free will survive in a person who is denied all political freedom? (In George Orwell's classic novel *Nineteen Eighty-Four*, the hero loses his will to think and feel for himself. Is this the ultimate destruction of a person – while allowing the associated human being to live?)

Hume's compatibilism

Must we sit in fear, awaiting news from scientists as to whether causal determinism is a reality? Should we dread the possibility of hearing that everything we do is causally determined? 'Not at all,' say those philosophers who are *compatibilists* about causal determinism and free will. They assure us that a person could think and act freely even if his or her thoughts and actions are caused by what has already occurred or been 'in place', even with no alternative thoughts and actions having been permitted by the world. But how could that be so?

Probably the most famous (although not the first) compatibilist reasoning was David Hume's. He argued that when people regard causal determinism ('necessity') as incompatible with our having free will ('liberty'), they confuse determinism with constraint. That is like confusing being guided and propelled with being compelled or impeded. The latter state of affairs is like being a *prisoner* – being constrained. But even a causally determined world does not restrict you in any way akin to being imprisoned. On the contrary: the world, with its causal patterns in place, is what enables you to think and act. It also guides and propels you; this is not your being compelled or impeded. For you are being given the underlying freedom to think and act in the first place. Indeed, a causally determined world is *required* if we are to think and act freely. If there were no causation within the world, there would be mere randomness instead. Indeterminism would reign. And that (as we saw in the section, Indeterminism), fails to be a metaphysical basis for thought and action.

Often (observed Hume), people think that the past has left open different possible actions for them to perform. So, they continue to believe that, because they are free, causal determinism does not obtain. But this thinking, claimed Hume, is traceable to people's not understanding the past well enough. We are unaware of the myriad details that combine to bring about whatever occurs, including our own actions. We should not infer, from our not understanding how something has been caused, that it has not been caused.

After all, asked Hume, don't we live by presuming that causation structures the world? Imagine your friends and family displaying no regular or understandable patterns of thought and behaviour. (And, as Chapter 10 (Hume on causation) will explain, for Hume causation is a matter of regular patterns obtaining.) If that were to persist for a long time, you might wonder whether something is amiss with your friends and family. Hume would regard their behaviour as random ('chance'), not free. Freedom worth having is like creativity worth having. Yes, it can be surprising; nonetheless, it is not a denial of determinism. It is built upon rigour, pattern, training. It is not mere wildness, randomness – which need not be anything more than indeterminism. (Hume called the latter 'chance … merely the negation of a cause'; and he doubted that it exists, because he thought that causality does so – in a sense which will be explained in Chapter 10 (Hume on causation).) Real freedom includes the ability to think or act controlledly or purposefully. The desire to be out of control can be fleetingly romantic. But it grounds nothing substantial, including one's character. ('He's just crazy – wild, unpredictable. He's great.' However, perhaps any such person is consistent or predictable in another way – predictably doing whatever his or her parents disapprove of, say. Could a person avoid all such predictability only by being so deeply inconsistent as to be acting genuinely crazily – a disturbing prospect?)

Hume also develops a similar compatibilism about causal determinism and moral responsibility. Is causal determinism a threat to the existence of moral responsibility? Not at all: the existence of a full causal order in the world is *required* if people are to be morally responsible for their actions. You are morally responsible for insulting Dave only if your doing so is caused by your character, your stable pattern of thoughts, feelings, motives, tendencies. Only then could you rightly be blamed for insulting him. In contrast, if you are forced by something external to insult Dave, you are being constrained – not just caused – to insult him; and this absolves you of blame. Or if you insult Dave without anything at all – including your own character, your own motives or preferences – causing this action, it remains unclear that you, strictly speaking, can rightly be blamed. Once more, therefore (Hume would have said), free will plus a rigorous causal history underlying your thoughts and actions is needed if you are to merit blame (or praise, for that matter) for what you think or do. And causal determinism in general is that rigorous causal order, applied to the world as a whole. Moral feelings – such as responses of outrage against a general injustice – are important to us, thought Hume. These rely upon assuming that a strict causality, rather than a loose randomness, structures the world – including our characters and thoughts and actions.

None of Hume's compatibilist claims depends on adopting a physicalist conception of persons. No matter whether a person is wholly physical, or wholly immaterial, or both physical and non-physical (these three possibilities having been considered in Chapter 1 (Physicalism, Immaterialism, Dualism)), causal patterns are present, Hume would say. And these patterns still help to define, rather than to preclude, our having free wills and our being morally responsible for our actions. That is how widely applicable Hume's compatibilist views are – if they are true.

Further reading

On free will and causal determinism in general:
  Gerald Dworkin (ed.), *Determinism, Free Will, and Moral Responsibility* (Englewood Cliffs, NJ: Prentice-Hall, 1970).
  John Martin Fischer, *The Metaphysics of Free Will: An Essay on Control* (Oxford: Blackwell, 1994).
  D.J. O'Connor, *Free Will* (Garden City, NY: Anchor Books, 1971).
  Richard Taylor, *Metaphysics*, 4th edn (Englewood Cliffs, NJ: Prentice-Hall, 1992), ch. 5.
  Peter van Inwagen, *Metaphysics*, 2nd edn (Boulder, CO: Westview Press, 2002), ch. 12.
  Gary Watson (ed.), *Free Will* (New York: Oxford University Press, 1982).

On fatalism:
  Steven M. Cahn, *Fate, Logic, and Time* (New Haven, CT: Yale University Press, 1967).
  Richard Taylor, *Metaphysics*, ch. 6.

On moral responsibility:
  John Martin Fischer and Mark Ravizza (eds), *Perspectives on Moral Responsibility* (Ithaca, NY: Cornell University Press, 1993).
  Harry G. Frankfurt, *The Importance of What We Care About: Philosophical Essays* (Cambridge: Cambridge University Press, 1988).

On foreknowledge:
  John Martin Fischer (ed.), *God, Foreknowledge, and Freedom* (Stanford, CA: Stanford University Press, 1989).

For Hume's compatibilism:
  David Hume, *An Enquiry Concerning Human Understanding*, sec. VIII.

3

God and Evil

The traditional problem of evil

When we think philosophically, our ultimate goal should include our explaining fundamental aspects of ourselves and the world. Should we therefore accept that there is a God? Many people would say so, maybe pointing to several reasons for that: 'Look around you. There is so much evidence of God's existence. Observe the world's complexity, its order – its apparent design. God created, and now sustains, the world. And read the Bible – it is clearly His word. Sometimes, too, I feel God's presence. He is why the world contains so much of value, such as the gift of life.'

Yet the world is not only order and beauty. It contains distressingly many cases of suffering, pain, degradation, and gross injustice. Much of this apparent evil – hardly too strong a word for it – is perpetrated by people against people. A great deal of it is often called natural evil, as winds, floods, earthquakes, and the like kill and maim and impoverish so effectively. (Living beings other than human beings are also affected in these ways. But philosophers tend not to discuss those cases of suffering.) How well – if at all – can we understand the existence of that apparent evil while conceiving of the world as being under the care of a mighty and loving God? Indeed, is the existence of evil a problem for our understanding the world at all? Why does even some evil exist?

To think about this more clearly, let's have in mind the case of Manda. I do not know her; she is fictional – except that, even as I write this, there is bound to be at least one young girl, somewhere in the world, whose life closely resembles Manda's. It is a life of ... well, Manda was abused sexually, violently and often, by her father; then she was sold into child labour, a form of slavery; she is about to be killed for trying to escape. She is only ten years old. What has she done to deserve such despicable treatment? The question is rhetorical; what else could it be? To interpret it in any other way would bespeak an indifference that is itself evil. Manda's life is horrid beyond belief; if your own child or sister or friend were to endure even one element of Manda's horrors, your sympathy and indignation would be real and resonant. The world contains many Mandas; why is there even one?

Later (in the section, Evil within people?), I will consider how we might begin answering that question if we were to relinquish a belief in God's existing. Before then, we may ask whether our knowing of such suffering as Manda's should *make* us relinquish that belief. This depends in part on what properties we believe God to possess. Various religions assure us that, regardless of whatever other properties God has, He is all-knowing (omniscient), all-good, and all-powerful (omnipotent). Yet how can such a God exist if the world houses Manda, living so blighted a life? That sort of question is at the core of the challenge called *the problem of evil*. In its simplest (and traditional) form, that challenge would say that Manda's existence, being so ravaged, *proves* there to be no wholly good, supremely powerful, and completely knowing God.

Here is the reasoning at the heart of that problem of evil:

> An all-knowing God would have known whatever was happening to Manda. And an all-good God would wish to prevent whatever suffering comes to His attention. So, an all-knowing and all-good God would wish to free Manda from her pain. But a God whose power is unlimited can put any of His wishes into effect. Hence, an all-knowing and all-good and all-powerful God would have made Manda's life free of the pain it has contained (and, for that matter, is about to contain). Yet Manda's life has manifestly not been free of that pain. Consequently, there is no such God.

In short, because seemingly needless suffering exists, the traditional problem of evil – presented, most famously, by Hume – concludes that there is no God.

Question 3.1   Is an action evil only if people deem it so? Or could it be evil without people believing that it is? Could the same action be evil – genuinely evil, rather than merely inappropriate – in one setting and not in another? If one culture's rulers or political leaders do not condemn a man for what another culture would abhor as his raping a young girl, is the man's action not evil within that culture? And if it is not evil there, is it not evil elsewhere? Or can even widely accepted aspects of a culture be evil? Will all cultures have evil aspects? Would any world not containing people also not include evil?

The world as a whole

Contemporary theistic philosophers deny that the traditional problem of evil *proves* there to be no all-good, all-powerful, and all-knowing God.

Yes, God would know what was happening to Manda; yes, God is all-good and all-powerful; but no (they insist), there remains a possibility of His not both wishing, and being able, to prevent Manda's pain and indignity.

This is because it is possible (say those theists) that even God's being wholly good and perfectly powerful does not include both His wishing and being able to prevent each *individual* piece of suffering, such as Manda's. God's having those properties might have required Him only to create a world that is morally good *as a whole*. He would have needed only to avoid creating a world that is morally deficient *overall*. So, even if we believe that Manda's life is almost too sad for words, it does not follow that God should have wished, and been able, to bring about a world from which Manda's pain is absent. Maybe eliminating her suffering would have made the world as a whole a morally poor one. How is that possible? We do not know for sure (admit these theists): we lack God's complete knowledge of this world's intricacies, not to mention His knowledge of each aspect of every alternative possible world He might have created instead of this one. We do not have God's perspective. We do not know His plan for the world. Whatever happens, therefore, could be part of a morally good outcome as a whole; we cannot know for sure that it is not.

At best, that theistic reply shows that the traditional problem of evil has not *proved* there to be no God. However, is that reply vulnerable to the following reasoning?

> To the extent that (by lacking God's perspective) we do not understand *how* whatever happens is part of a morally good outcome for the world as a whole, we also fail to know that whatever happens *is* part of some such outcome – or, therefore, that whatever happens is part of some such outcome being overseen by God.

For example (continues that reasoning), we would weaken our rational right to believe that God both cares about, and oversees, any specific individual's well-being. If we claim only that God would create and maintain a world that is morally good *overall*, we cannot know that God both cares about, and is responsible for, your *particular* good fortune. After all, the theistic defence conceded that God could not be known both to care about, and be able to prevent, your particular *mis*fortune. Might atheists therefore welcome that concession by theists?

Question 3.2 Can theistic people be as cruel and thoughtless as anyone else? Does believing that there is a God guarantee one's being sensitive to other people's suffering? Is there any link between people believing that there is a God and the world's being less evil? Some people claim, or are said, to be spiritual; could such a person nonetheless be selfish and hard-hearted? If so, what – if anything – is the moral importance in being deemed to be spiritual?

The evidence-problem of evil

Regardless of whether or not the existence of pronounced pain and suffering *proves* that there is no all-good, all-powerful, and all-knowing God, is it nonetheless *very good evidence* of there being no such God? If so, then even if (as the section, The world as a whole, wondered) the traditional problem of evil does not prove what it claims to prove, there remains an *evidence-problem* of evil.

Manda's is a striking case. But the history of humanity is awash with cases of inhumanity. It is routine – quite properly – to cite the indignities and worse that were imposed upon Jews (among others) by Nazi Germany. Hitler is far from alone, however, within the category of those who have overseen widespread torture, slaughter, and degradation, usually on political or ideological grounds. Just reflect upon Stalin in the Soviet Union, as well as Mao in China, then Pol Pot in Cambodia, Idi Amin in Uganda, Mobutu in (what was then) Zaire, Chile's Pinochet, and upon South African apartheid – and realise that these rulers or regimes have been merely some of the sources of horror for millions of people within just one century. Start reading about previous centuries and other countries, too; where does it end?

No more evidence (many thinkers will aver) is needed of there being no perfectly good and powerful and knowing God. Corporate criminals, with their often glaring and vile indifference towards those whose lives their greed can so easily ruin; racist lynchings; religious wars; and so on: it is true that the world could have been worse, yet seemingly it might have been much better. The good evidence of these kinds of moral badness that the world has contained is also good evidence of how the world as a whole might have been morally better than it is. The previous section's theistic response would note that even all of that apparent moral badness is not *conclusive* evidence of the world's being somewhat morally deficient; nonetheless (we should ask), is it still *good* evidence of that deficiency within the world? If so, it is thereby good evidence of there being no all-good, all-powerful, and all-knowing God. ('But how could evidence be good without being conclusive – without being a proof?' Chapter 8 (Fallibilism) will explain how.)

A theist might reply to that reasoning, however, by saying that we do not have even good evidence of the world's being at all morally deficient, unless we have good evidence of at least some of that suffering being morally needless. And do we? People sometimes improve as persons – becoming more tolerant or patient or empathetic, say – by undergoing or witnessing hardship. Is *all* suffering a necessary step towards people's developing qualities that contribute to the world's moral goodness? If so, then no suffering is needless; it could look needless, without really being so. Presumably, we would rarely, if ever, know *why* a particular piece of pain is not needless. We would not even know that Manda's suffering has been incurred for no ultimately morally triumphant reason. To say that Manda's plight is good evidence of there being no all-good, all-powerful, and all-knowing God is to say that we have good evidence that her pain is not part of whatever plan such a God would have for us, for instance. And how could we have good evidence of that?

Central to that theistic reply to the claimed evidence-problem of evil is a fundamental issue about how to interpret our observations of the world. We observe people, apparently in pain; perhaps we do not always observe there being a morally good reason for that pain. Do we thereby observe the pain's being needless – serving no morally sufficient purpose within the world as a whole? Or must we use our powers of reason, too, if we are to understand the world in that way? *Can* we do that? (In Chapters 10 through to 12, our capacity to understand – to know – the world by observing and thinking will be examined.)

So, we confront a basic question about rational belief:

> Is there *better* evidence for the existence of a God than there is against a God's existing? In particular, does our knowledge of some or all of the world's pain and suffering rationally outweigh whatever evidence we might claim to possess of God's existing?

('Who is ever to say, though, which evidence is good and which is not?' This question is beside the immediate point, as we will appreciate in Chapter 8.)

Question 3.3   Whenever people do not deeply care about the evil done to others, is this an evil in itself? Is the fact of people often saying that they care – when really they do not – a further evil? Does evil exist whenever people wish to lessen others' pain only after it has occurred, instead of trying to prevent it to begin with (even if this would mean having less wealth and privilege themselves)? Mother Teresa of Calcutta provided shelter for ailing poor people; there is good evidence that she refused them medical care, though (either preventive or curative), because she deemed their suffering to be God's will. Was that presumptuous, and less caring than it could have been, on her part?

The free will defence

We have been asking whether the world, with its apparent evil, could ultimately be due to a God who is all-knowing, all-powerful, and all-good. If we are to take seriously the possibility of explaining the world theistically, therefore, we seek a way of *understanding* why some or all of the world's evil occurs (while continuing to believe that there is a God). What is generally known as *the free will defence* does indeed claim to explain, in a theistic way, some of the world's evil:

> In His goodness, God has given people free wills. It is not His fault when we misuse our free wills in ways that harm others. Evil that is freely performed by us is not God's fault.

Manda's pain is due to her being exploited by other people, who exercise their own free wills in mistreating her. The evil they thereby cause is their fault, not God's.

How philosophically effective is the free will defence? I will mention three questions about its scope and strength.

Natural evil   Are all deaths of people via earthquakes, floods, cyclones, and so on, due to the misuse of free will? Admittedly, increased deforestation of hillsides – a series of actions, perhaps performed freely – can make a flood more deadly. But only some deaths in some floods (and let us not forget earthquakes, cyclones, and the like) are at all due to such uses of free will. 'No, it is all due to us. Because people freely sin, God punishes people. It is against His nature to punish people arbitrarily.' So, whenever people – including babies – drown in a flood, did they deserve that death because they were sinners?

Surrounding circumstances   When people use their free wills to achieve outcomes they desire, generally they depend on surrounding circumstances being apt. No one rationally expects that, regardless of how the world around us is, everything we freely attempt will succeed. (We are not that powerful; effective personal development includes one's knowing this.) However, if God is all-knowing, He knows which circumstances would allow which acts of free will to have their intended effects. And if God is all-powerful, couldn't He affect the surrounding circumstances whenever a person is freely acting in a way that would – if not interrupted – cause needless pain? Couldn't God do this without depriving people of their free wills as such? If so, couldn't He affect those surrounding circumstances so that free uses of our wills have no evil results? For example, on each occasion when Manda's father had freely decided to abuse her, God might have caused some small event to occur which would have prevented Manda's father from satisfying those freely formed desires. (Or would such interventions by God make Manda's father's will unfree? How free – how powerful – are our wills?) If God had always intervened like this throughout history, maybe people's free wills would not have been used over time to hurt others. Perhaps people would have freely stopped trying to act in those ways; they would willingly have found alternative – non-harmful – ways of acting freely. So, even if the free will defence does explain why God is not morally responsible for a person's exercising his or her free will in a way that will – provided that nothing intervenes – cause others grief, would God still be morally responsible – by not causing anything to intervene – for the world's being such that those exercises of free will have those grievous consequences? If so, would God be at least partly morally responsible for the evil caused by people using their free wills?

God's foreknowledge   Is the free will defence available to us if we claim that God is all-knowing? Consider the following interrelated questions (each one outlining possible implications of a pertinent supposition).

1. In Chapter 2 (Foreknowledge) we asked whether, if God always knows in advance what people are about to do, none of our actions are free. But if God's having such foreknowledge has that result, does it imply the failure of the free will defence? Would God be morally responsible for the evil which He foresees people causing – yet which they do not freely cause?

2. Suppose, instead, that God does not know in advance what people will do. But suppose that this lack of knowledge on God's part is due to there being no regularities or patterns in people's behaviour. Then maybe (as Chapter 2 (Indeterminism, Hume's compatibilism) suggested) people would not be acting freely – given that mere random movements are not free actions. And would the free will defence thereby fail? Would God be morally responsible for whatever evil is not freely – because it is indeterministically – done by people?

3. Suppose that although God does not know in advance what people will do, this is not because they act randomly. Instead, there are regularities and patterns in their behaviour (and so they might be acting freely). In that case, however, because God fails (even given the good evidence provided by those regularities and patterns) to know in advance what people are going to do, God is not all-knowing. So, there would be no all-knowing, all-good, and all-powerful God.

In one way or another, therefore, does the free will defence prevent our understanding the world by including in our story a conception of God as being all-knowing, all-good, and all-powerful?

Question 3.4 Often, people to whom life has been generous encourage those to whom it has been less bountiful, such as those living in poverty, to accept their fate as being God's will – and therefore as being unalterable. Might that be suspiciously convenient thinking by those comparatively (and generally arbitrarily) privileged people? Might it contribute to their not regarding themselves as being insensitive if they do not help the disadvantaged people? Could a belief in God's existence thus entrench, or even increase, economic and social hardship in the world?

Socrates's challenge

A great number of people think that if there is no God then nothing is either evil or morally good. If we were not to believe that there is an all-good, all-powerful, and all-knowing God, would we be rationally obliged to relinquish belief in morality – in there being moral truths? Would we have no explanation of the world's moral aspects? 'Perhaps, therefore, given the existence of marked and widespread suffering which we believe to be an evil, we should infer, not that there is no God, but instead that there *is* a God.' We would thus turn the problem of evil 'on its head' – saying that if some actions are evil, they thereby have a sort of property that would not exist if there were no God. In that way (we would conclude), only a belief that there is a God protects us from accepting moral lawlessness and anarchy – the emptiness of our concepts of moral goodness and evil. So, is it morally irresponsible not to believe that there is a God?

An ancient argument, presented by one of the greatest thinkers, disputes that way of reasoning. The argument is in the *Euthyphro*, one of the many dialogues written by the Greek philosopher Plato (429–347 BC) which have been foundational to much subsequent Western thought. The main character in this Platonic dialogue, as in almost all of them, is Plato's brilliant teacher Socrates (469–399 BC). The argument in question was Socrates's. He was talking to a religious man, Euthyphro, about what makes an action morally good. Euthyphro was confident of his views (as were most people before they had been talking to Socrates for long). He claimed that morally good actions are those of which the gods approve; the gods' approval makes an action morally good. But (asked Socrates) is that quite right? Is an action morally good because it is approved of by the gods? Or is it approved of by the gods because it is morally good? Euthyphro conceded that the latter, not the former, is true. It is not the gods' approval as such that we should venerate; their approval is valuable only insofar as it directs us to what is worthy of approval. Not everyone's approval of an action would direct us unfailingly; presumably a god's would, though, because only a god would so reliably – indeed, unfailingly – know whether a particular action is worthy of approval. Only a god could ascertain completely accurately what the action is like in itself, along with all surrounding circumstances. Only a god would know for sure whether the action is one of which we should approve. Consequently, the gods' approving of the action is a perfect indicator of its being a morally good action; their approving of it does not *make* it a morally good action.

If Socrates was right, then, there is the possibility of an action's having a moral quality – being evil, being morally good – independently of its being approved of by the gods. (For instance, a rape undoubtedly includes the victim's feelings of powerlessness and pain and despair, along with the rapist's callousness. Presumably these feelings are morally relevant features of the situation in itself. Are they already enough to make the rape immoral?) And Socrates would probably say the same about a single God; philosophers have generally thought of his argument as implying about God what he claimed it shows about the gods. Is it therefore possible that our actions could have moral qualities even if no God exists? To establish this possibility does not prove that there are moral qualities in the world. But it does show that if there are some, this need not be because there exists a God. Hence, it reveals the possibility of taking a crucial first step towards a non-religious ethics.

Question 3.5   Can a person become better at being ethical? Is acting morally a skill? If so, is being unethical – even evil – also a skill? Might a group of people develop better ethical skills? Might a group lose those skills? How might a person's not believing that there is a God help to make him or her more ethical than one who does believe there to be a God? Conversely, how might believing that there is a God help to make a person more ethical?

Evil within people?

In case there is no God, or in case there need not be a God if the world is to include some evil, we should seek to explain *how* there could be evil even if there is no God. In particular, let's reflect a little upon the genesis of some of the evil that people perpetrate against people. Why does such evil occur? Is it due to aspects of the world beyond ourselves – for instance, historical or social forces? Or might some – even all – of it emanate from within us? Maybe there are features of how people think and feel that make us more likely to treat others badly, given opportunities to do so. (Possibly, too, these characteristics are ones that people – with some timely self-knowledge – could lessen within themselves, thereby lowering that likelihood.)

Such features might be surprisingly subtle. They can also be unremarkable, everyday. Evil is not confined to deranged psychopaths or ranting rabid bigots – spectacularly afflicted people. You or I or anyone else could treat others badly. Why are some people particularly prone to doing so?

There have been psychological experiments (most famously and controversially by Stanley Milgram at Yale University in the 1960s) testing how readily people will, when told to do so, perform actions that they believe are inflicting pain – even serious pain – upon others. Worryingly, most people in the experiments were only too willing to acquiesce. Why was that so? Why did their other features not counteract what seems to have been those people's ready subservience to authority?

Maybe these people did not possess sufficiently strongly what are sometimes termed *the human responses*. These are ways of having deep feelings of the reality of others' humanity. (There is a difference between acknowledging each other's humanity and feeling it emotionally.) For example, there is the instinct of treating other people with *respect*, not putting on airs, not seeking to belittle or 'look past' or 'look through' them. There is also the instinct of *sympathy* – where this is a full feeling, not a mere platitude. It takes little imagination to appreciate how anyone in whom these instincts are present only weakly is more likely, all else being equal, to act uncaringly or inhumanely towards others.

It takes a little more imagination to notice indications in everyday life of someone's having those instincts less firmly than is desirable. It is important to be aware of which characteristics of people, even as they live their usual lives in standard circumstances, could – particularly if unusual circumstances were to arise – easily lead to their treating others in degrading or harmful ways. I do not know for sure that the following two human characteristics are like that. But it could be revealing to ask whether they might be. (And if they are not, are *other* aspects of us like that?)

Representations of violence   A vast number of people clearly like, or do not mind, seeing depictions, within movies or television shows, of extreme violence or degradation. 'But it's not real,' most say when responding to the question of how they can view such scenes without revulsion. Yet in some respects it might as well be real. It looks real; and at any moment, such scenes of torture or maiming or killing are occurring somewhere in the world. (Imagine seeing a film that you believe is a fictional representation of a torture – and then being told that it is a documentary. Would you only then feel disgusted at what you have seen? Morally, shouldn't you *already* have had that feeling in response to those images?) When New York's World Trade Center buildings were destroyed by terrorists in 2001, suddenly Hollywood film companies did not want to show, and people did not want to see, movies portraying kindred events. This did not bespeak any deep morality; such films had routinely been made and enjoyed until then. If buildings had been destroyed in the same way in New Delhi, for example, would Hollywood have reacted as it did? Would Indians' suffering have mattered to Hollywood? (It is never difficult for people to react 'morally' when those from 'their own group' are treated unjustly. However, that is at best a superficial morality if those people do not acknowledge the same moral urgency whenever similar injustice is suffered by people from some 'other' group.)

I am not suggesting that in everyday circumstances many people who enjoy or tolerate on-screen violence will recreate those scenes of violence. But a basic human response of sympathy might well be deficient in anyone responding like that to such portrayals. They can witness such images without revulsion or shock, at least when the images are not of pain or injustice being incurred by people they know or with whom they identify. And that is a step towards being able to tolerate some people being treated like that if less benign circumstances were to take shape around them. (Think of the terrible treatment of Jews by so much of the population in Nazi Germany, or the ritualised humiliation and worse that became common in Mao's China, for example. Could such events ever occur in your own country? Why not – if your fellow citizens' instincts do not recoil sufficiently strongly, at a time when no insidious social movements are affecting your country, from representations of such behaviour? People routinely assure themselves and others that they would never act in those ways; how good is their evidence for that self-congratulatory confidence?)

Casual insensitivity Watch people around you (and, for that matter, try to be aware of your own behaviour) when walking in a city or a busy shopping centre. Look at faces. Be aware of people who are insensitive to other pedestrians, who presume that *others* will always make way for *them*, who seem to regard themselves as more important than others within that setting. Many faces look like they really do not care, when all is said and done, about the welfare of others. (Be cautious in scrutinising people in this way, of course. It can be hard to interpret faces accurately.) Now imagine those same personal characteristics within less relaxed circumstances. For instance, sometimes – for nothing more admirable than short-term electoral advantages – politicians play upon people's insecurities regarding a population's ethnic mix. Rhetoric like this might be used: 'They will take over our country, our suburbs, with their different ways of living – their gangs, their distrust of us. But together we can keep them out.' And maybe such rhetoric is sometimes effective because, for all too many people, it is easy to cease viewing those with different ethnic lineages from their own as being people with feelings, reactions, values, and concerns substantially like their own. ('A mother from that country wouldn't feel as strongly about her child as we do about ours.') See how readily evil within a society can be encouraged – including indifference to, or cowardice in the presence of, violent or unjust measures being implemented by others.

Further reading

On the traditional problem of evil:

Marilyn McCord Adams and Robert Merrihew Adams (eds), *The Problem of Evil* (New York: Oxford University Press, 1990).

David Hume, *Dialogues Concerning Natural Religion*, Part X.

J.L. Mackie, *The Miracle of Theism: Arguments For and Against the Existence of God* (Oxford: Clarendon Press, 1982), ch. 9.

Richard Swinburne, *The Existence of God*, rev. edn (Oxford: Clarendon Press, 1991), chs 9–11.

On the evidence-problem of evil:

Daniel Howard-Snyder (ed.), *The Evidential Argument from Evil* (Bloomington, IN: Indiana University Press, 1996).

On the free will defence:

Alvin Plantinga, *God, Freedom, and Evil* (New York: Harper & Row, 1974), Part I.

For Socrates's challenge:

Plato, *Euthyphro*, 10d–11b.

On the apparent evil within us:

Jonathan Glover, *Humanity: A Moral History of the Twentieth Century* (London: Jonathan Cape, 1999).

Ronald D. Milo, *Immorality* (Princeton, NJ: Princeton University Press, 1984).

Richard Taylor, *Good and Evil* (Amherst, NY: Prometheus Books, 2000 [1970]), chs 14–17.

4

Life's Meaning

Criteria of meaning?

Is human life inherently meaningful? Let's think about individual human lives: maybe some are meaningful while others are not; possibly a life is meaningful at some times and not at others. What – if anything – can ever impart meaning to a person's life? To answer that question, we must ascertain which *criteria* to apply; otherwise, vagueness abounds. In this section, I mention two general criteria. (These underlie the more specific ideas discussed in the rest of this chapter.)

You might suggest, for example, that happiness makes a life meaningful. But this depends, for a start, upon whether meaning must be a 'higher' aspect of one's life (since happiness as such is not clearly like that):

The depth question How deep or profound must a life's meaning be? Is meaning available only to people – perhaps only to special or distinctive people? (Is there no meaning in a toad's life? What of an elephant's? What about 'ordinary' people's lives?)

Now reflect on a life of suffering that results in an insightful and widely used book – published posthumously. We might accord that life a 'higher' meaning, because it was thoughtful and it helped many others. However, was it meaningful if the author never thought of it in that way – never experiencing it as being meaningful? Here is the more general question behind that one:

The obviousness question Is it always obvious whether or not one's life has meaning? (Whenever you believe that your life is meaningful, either overall or in some particular respect, will you be correct? Whenever meaning is present in your life, will you believe – notice – that it is?)

Notably, many 'motivational speakers' and 'inspirational celebrities' would have us believe that meaning is present within our lives whenever we decide that it is:

> There is meaning in your life if you think there is. It can be whatever you deem
> or wish it to be. In this way, with your mind, you can control this dimension of
> your life. It is up to you to make your life meaningful – and yes, you can do this!

Yet too optimistic a view of oneself might encompass one's ignoring
one's limitations and failures within the world. Is it possible to think
highly of oneself without rationally deserving to do so? Is life's meaning never simply one's having high self-esteem? Even when you know
what you are feeling, you might not know whether that feeling makes
your life meaningful. It is possible that we are only imperfect judges of
what, if anything, gives our lives meaning. Accordingly, it is possible
that meaning within a life is not always apparent; it could have the
potential to be partly or wholly *hidden*. Might your life seem meaningless to you, in general or in some respect, even while an aspect of it con-
tributes meaning without your realising this? More disturbingly, could
your life seem meaningful to you, as a whole or in a particular respect,
while actually lacking meaning?

Question 4.1   Might someone else understand better than you do what meaning,
if any, your life contains? What characteristics would such a person need? Do your
parents have such insight? What of your friends? Will only someone other than
you have sufficient 'distance' or 'detachment'? Or can no one understand what
does, or does not, make another's life meaningful? Are onlookers always *too*
'distant' or 'detached'? (But if you – as an onlooker – cannot understand whether
other people's lives have meaning, might you never understand whether your own
life has some? Would you have no standards of comparison based on understanding the meaning, or lack of it, within another's life?)

The myth of Sisyphus

One potential way of discovering which (if any) properties can make
a life meaningful is by thinking about a life from which meaning is
absent – and asking what could be added to that life to give it some
meaning.

Is a meaningless life possible? Philosophers have often regarded the
ancient Greek myth of Sisyphus as describing such a life. Day after day,
Sisyphus toils. He does so forever, no escape being possible. The gods
had ordained that – unto eternity – his life consists of his doing just one
thing, repeatedly. He pushes a rock up a hill. Then it rolls back down.
He pushes it up the hill again – whereupon it rolls back down. He
pushes ... on and on, ceaselessly. In effect, Sisyphus is a slave, living
much as many actual people still do, such as in so-called labour camps
in assorted countries. ('You've dug that ditch. Now fill it in – then dig

it again.') His is a dire life. But I will describe some conceivable changes to it. Will any of these give it meaning?

Pleasure   Suppose that Sisyphus happens to want to be doing what he is doing. He even rejoices in his labours being endless and unvaried. Would he be satisfying a desire worth satisfying, though? It might be thought that his experiences of pleasure would be deeply irrational. ('It's crazy – literally – to enjoy doing that.') And presumably few, if any, deeply irrational lives are clearly meaningful. (Or – given the circumstances – would it be an *achievement* for Sisyphus to experience that pleasure?)

You might reply, '*My* desires are not irrational. The lack of meaning in Sisyphus's satisfying his desires does not detract from the meaning in my satisfying mine.' But what if satisfying pleasures is not meaningful anyway? Maybe it is just … pleasurable – which is just … satisfying. People tend not to think that if a cat feels pleasure, its life is thereby meaningful. So, when next you hear them enthusing about the meaning provided in their lives by 'good food, good wine, good conversation – sheer pleasure', ask yourself whether it is obvious that their lives are thereby more meaningful than a happy cat's. Is pleasure as such somehow too superficial to contribute real meaning to a life?

Money   Picture Sisyphus being paid money – even a lot of it – for his labours. Each time he reaches the top of the hill, fresh money awaits him. There are those who regard money as inherently meaningful. (I have heard it called spiritual!) Or is the money's presence too shallow to be making Sisyphus's life at all meaningful? ('Money is meaningful because of what we can do with it.' Suppose that, at the base of the hill, Sisyphus uses the money to make purchases, including ones he covets. It is far from obvious that this makes his life meaningful.)

Companionship   Imagine Sisyphus's not being alone: he shares the hill with several other people, similarly condemned. (Some of these people could be his friends; possibly, some are members of his family – kinfolk.) Is there nonetheless no meaning in living like Sisyphus or his fellow toilers – no matter that one would not be a solitary toiler? There might not always be meaning in companionship (even when there is pleasure). Must the wider setting also be apt?

Free will   Perhaps Sisyphus exercises some free will. He chooses how quickly to walk and which direction to follow; he decides what to think about and whether to sing; maybe there are TVs on the hill which he can elect to watch as he proceeds. However, might these possibilities be insufficiently deep to contribute meaning to Sisyphus's life? ('But what if he uses his free will to decide to enjoy his life?' He would be like those people who seek to alter their attitudes towards what they cannot change within their lives, believing that by coming to embrace what formerly they had resisted, they create meaning where previously there was none: 'I'm going to view it positively from now on.' Do they succeed in creating meaning? Answering that question will return us to the first suggestion.)

Achievement   At present, Sisyphus's actions seem rather insignificant, achieving nothing. So, suppose that, at the top of the hill, he slowly creates a building that helps other people. Yet is a prisoner's life meaningful because – while imprisoned – he or she creates something that happens to help others? ('It depends on whether the prisoner – while wishing not to be imprisoned – wants to be creating some such thing.' Does this thinking, too, return us to the first suggestion?)

Complexity   Finally, we may picture Sisyphus's life as having more than one of the above properties. Indeed, let all of them be present. His life thereby becomes quite varied, interestingly complex. Perhaps he creates a building; he is paid for doing so; he has some choice in how he does so; he enjoys himself; he has companionship; and so on. But is even this enough to make his life meaningful? After all, he remains trapped, still rolling rocks.

Now we should think about our own lives. If Sisyphus's life never ceases being meaningless (even as it becomes more complex), should we worry about whether our own lives are ever meaningful? For Sisyphus – his life enlivened and enriched by those imagined distractions and details – would be living in a way with some similarity to how many actual people live. If even the most 'sophisticated' Sisyphean life remains meaningless, perhaps many or all of our own lives – generally enlivened by comparable variety – are also meaningless. Do we fill our lives with much that – no matter how enjoyable and socially respectable – fails to make them meaningful? It depends on whether there is an *underlying* pointlessness to our lives – as there possibly is in Sisyphus's – depriving us of any deeper form of meaning. We need to reflect on whether our lives might have some such failing, even if we never notice or feel its presence. Can we make our lives meaningful in ways that are unavailable to Sisyphus? How can we 'rise above' a Sisyphean life?

Question 4.2   When are repetitiveness and boredom necessary to creativity? 'Never. Being creative is about letting one's mind run free, unshackled by the world.' But doesn't your mind – even if non-physical – remain limited in what it can accomplish? Will these limitations exist, even if you cannot feel them? Do such limitations make your life less significant or meaningful? Is significance or meaning a matter of 'breaking free', feeling unconstrained? Or is it more a matter of what you actually do with your actual abilities? Is creativity more than feeling creative?

Plato's cave

Imagine Sisyphus believing himself to be blessed with an important and enviable lifestyle. He would therefore be badly ignorant about his role in the world. Would this make his life more pitiful than it already is? His thinking so well of his life could even – without his realising it – render him a figure of fun. (Dignity requires accuracy in one's sense of oneself.)

Another of philosophy's enduring images is rather like that. Usually called the parable of the cave, it comes from the *Republic*, one of Plato's dialogues. The parable is a story of people unknowingly imprisoned. Always having dwelt in a cave, chained there, they never experience the world outside – without knowing of this lack of theirs. They are content with their lives – without realising that there is an important respect in which they should not be. They even have satisfying social lives with each other. They take life's potential to begin and end with what is possible for them within the cave. If you were to enter the cave, telling them that it does not exhaust the realm of the real, you would be ignored or ridiculed. These people's happiness is that of the ignorant: their understanding of the world is sadly lacking. They are misleadingly satisfied with themselves and their conception of reality. They are deeply ignorant – even of being deeply ignorant.

Why does Plato tell us about these people? The reason is chilling: 'They are us,' he says. They are us, so long as we are content to live everyday lives, knowing nothing beyond 'the passing show'. If that is how we live, we lack something vital. We remain chained in a cave ourselves. We are deeply ignorant – even of being deeply ignorant.

'No, that is not *our* plight. We are confident that we understand our capacities and the world.' Is such confidence mistaken, though? Do we often live at least aspects of our lives inside 'lesser' Platonic caves – through devotion to a business or company, a family, a culture, a country, and so on? This is not to say that any such narrow focus is automatically meaningless. But might it lack meaning (in the way Plato described) *if* the narrow focus results in our not realising how unaware we are of much of the world? (A company boss might know only about his or her part of an economy, all the while confident of being well-placed to opine on the economy as a whole; an economist will possibly not appreciate how simplified are his or her models of economic reality; a politician could continually compromise his or her apparent attempts to reflect accurately upon the economy or society or even upon people, focussed more on being re-elected than on being correct; and so on.) There is a multitude of ways for us not to notice how little we know about the world, with our thinking being unwittingly narrow.

Are those also ways for our lives to be that much less meaningful – without our being aware of it? They are – if being badly misled about reality makes us less 'in touch with', or 'connected to', ourselves and the world. This is especially so when our ignorance is of fundamental features. Might you fail to understand your own nature – no matter that it is yours? Might you misjudge your capacities for knowing the nature of the world – no matter that you live in it? Ascertaining whether we have those flaws is central to this book. We began by asking what it is to be a person, trying to understand ourselves. In later chapters we will ask what knowledge is – and how much, if any, we have. Without such understanding, we do not understand whether our lives have meaning – or whether, instead, we are fairly represented by those unfortunates in Plato's cave. But, Plato would say, to lack such understanding is to guarantee that one *is* living inside the cave. Is he right? If so, maybe a deep kind of knowledge – of oneself and the wider world – is necessary for a meaningful life.

Question 4.3   Is a religious life meaningful if its fundamental beliefs about the nature of the world – including the belief that there is a God – are false? Would it be a badly deluded life? (I am not saying that there is no God; I am considering a possibility.) Is a life of helping other people meaningful only if not based on a belief that one will eventually be rewarded (even if in a 'next life') for living like that? Is a life of 'withdrawing from the world' (perhaps praying and meditating, being financially supported by a church bureaucracy) a meaningless life, especially if based on false beliefs? Can secular lives – including both intellectual ones and anti-intellectual ones – be valueless, too, if centred upon false beliefs? Is seeking truth part of seeking meaning? Is seeking meaning sufficient for having meaning?

Nozick's machines

The American philosopher Robert Nozick (1938–2002) imagined three machines – an *experience* machine, a *transformation* machine, and a *result* machine. There they are (we may suppose), arrayed before you. Here is what you must choose to do – or not:

Have yourself plugged into any of them, if you wish!

The experience machine gives you whatever experiences you wish to have for the next two years, say. (In contemporary terms, it is a 'virtual reality' machine.) The transformation machine turns you into any sort of person you wish to be (short of the qualitatively new person no longer being numerically identical to you). And the result machine brings about whatever you could realistically wish to bring about in the world: it allows you to 'make a difference' to the world. Your brain gets plugged into a machine; then you recline in a tank, lazing away the ensuing minutes, months, or years. What could be better than that? If you believe that meaning is present within any life that includes various kinds of experience (including 'virtual' ones), or within any life that is available only to a particular kind of person, or within a life that makes the world significantly different, then shouldn't you reach eagerly for those machines?

'Not at all,' Nozick would say. He assumes that people would refuse the invitation to be 'plugged-in'. He seems to think that to be plugged-in is to lessen the living of one's own life as such. How might that be so? Nozick provides no detailed analysis.

But here is one idea (as we continue seeking an understanding of what meaning could be): Possibly, there is no meaning in a life that can be controlled so effectively. Many people find repellent the possibility of being causally determined 'from outside' (as described in Chapter 2 (Determinism)). They might think that this would make living meaningless. Still, regardless of whether they are right about that, maybe our lives would lack meaning if we were to control them in advance *ourselves*.

Why might such control be incompatible with meaning? Again, it depends on what meaning involves. One possible dimension of meaning that we have not discussed is that of personal struggle *and hope*. Sisyphus struggles; but he can never triumph, escaping his underlying fate – and he knows this already. Insofar as he knows whatever will happen in his life, he cannot live in hope of something else occurring. Might our own lives be meaningless when hope either does or should depart? Hope does depart when the feeling of hope goes. Hope should depart whenever its still being present as a feeling is only because one is ignoring facts which render hope futile and of which one should be aware. And one circumstance in which it can be futile for you to hope that some specific event will occur is when that event has already clearly occurred or when you already know that it will occur.

Hence, insofar as you can control your life via Nozick's machines, you should abandon your hopes. For you cannot still hope to achieve something that you have already achieved, or that you already know you will achieve. And you already know that Nozick's machines will bring about your achieving whatever you wish to achieve by using them. Accordingly, being plugged into one of his machines should drive away all associated hopes.

Usually, when hope does depart, this is because of 'external' forces or circumstances which we believe we cannot control. But does Nozick's thought-experiment reveal that life would be meaningless if we *were* to control our lives as much as we might wish to do so and if we *were* to know perfectly what our lives will include? We would probably not feel or notice that lack of meaning; might the meaning be absent anyway? (By analogy: If causal determinism were to obtain, we need not notice its doing so. Yet many people claim that it would remain an underlying 'lessening' of us.)

A vast number of people forage for complete certainty, perfect knowledge, along with ways of controlling their minds, their bodies, other people, society, even the world. (Many seek gurus or advisers who cater to these dreams of complete knowledge and control.) However, there might be a deep danger in such quests: Would your attaining complete knowledge and control *deprive* your life of related meaning (even if you would not notice this lack)? For when there is total knowledge and control, all related hopes should depart. (They usually do not. But they should, as the previous three paragraphs explained.) May we therefore take from Nozick's story the moral that you have meaning within your life only if there is some imperfection in your attempts to know and to control your life? ('I don't want total control, though. I would choose to be plugged into the experience machine, requesting some unpredictability in my subsequent experiences.' Yet you would control this lack of control; you would know completely of your not knowing all the details. You would have full knowledge and control of your life's being less predictable than it would otherwise have been.) The suggestion, then, is that there is no meaning for your life in attaining a desired outcome if you gain it by completely knowing and controlling how it will occur. (Many people think of love, say, as contributing to a life's meaning. How could there be real meaning in a supposedly romantic relationship if you were to control it fully? And could you know every aspect of it only by controlling it fully?) Is this therefore a way in which it is never wholly obvious whether a particular life is meaningful? Meaning would be present only if one does not fully understand or control one's life – which then leaves open the possibility that one is mistaken as to whether meaning is present. Thus, whether one has a meaningful life would not be wholly obvious – even when one does have such a life.

Question 4.4   If there is no meaning to life, does this make people's lives unworthy of respect? 'Yes, I could treat other people however I wish, as nastily as I wish. Their suffering would not matter.' Yet in that same sense, would your desire to mistreat people also have no importance or merit – because *it* would be meaningless?

Need our thinking about life's meaning, or lack of it, be an essential part of our thinking about what is morally right or wrong? Or can there be moral rights and wrongs regardless of whether there are meaningful lives?

Living ethically

People often seek meaning within their lives by trying to act ethically: 'I used to have a shallow and selfish life; now it has gained meaning, because I'm trying to be ethically good.' It is somewhat of a conventional reflex to agree that a life lived more ethically is thereby deeper, ennobled. (I have that reflex myself.) But do we understand why that link exists, if indeed it does? And how strong a link would it be? *How* ethical must one be, if meaning is to be present in that way?

Presumably it is your being ethical, not your thereby satisfying a desire to be ethical, that would give your life meaning. How would even this occur, though? Suppose that Nozick's result machine (in the previous section) has a special setting called 'Happy World'. By activating the Happy World setting, you would – in an instant – eradicate all present and future misery from the world, eliminating any continuing need for pity and charity. Go ahead, then; make everyone's day – flick that switch! If this would be an ethically good action for you to perform, would doing so make your life meaningful? ('I remember the day I eliminated suffering from the world. Ever since, my life has meant something.')

Even this is not clear. Might there now be an emotional emptiness in your life, insofar as a desire to act ethically is a desire to *continue* doing so – and with all further need for ethical actions having disappeared? (For simplicity, we may assume that a need for ethical actions remains only if there still is, or might be, suffering in the world.) Perhaps you feel satisfied at your achievement. Yet is satisfaction meaningful in itself? And maybe there is no meaning in an achievement – even an ethical one – that is so easily attained. Possibly, an ongoing effort to be ethical is required – an ethical process, involving continued ethical actions. Are uncertainty, struggle, and ongoing commitment (themes we also encountered in the previous section) essential to whatever, if any, meaning is gained by acting ethically? Is a meaningful-because-ethical life a continuing and imperfect *effort*?

Question 4.5   Mustafa and Errol perform what is qualitatively the same job. But they live in different countries, in only one of which is that job well-paid. Does one of Mustafa and Errol therefore have a more meaningful life (all else being equal) than the other does? Or is one of their lives simply more fortunate than the other? If we seek to improve the living conditions of the poorly-paid man by contributing to aid programmes, does this make our lives more meaningful? Does it not do so if those aid programmes fail? ('Well, I tried!') Do you contribute to others' lives being meaningful, only insofar as you act ethically towards them?

Living philosophically

Often, people's struggles and uncertainties are philosophical, sometimes unwittingly so. It is possible to live quite philosophically, seeking real understanding of oneself and the world. This involves thinking about philosophical topics – such as the nature of persons, how people should treat each other, what injustice is, or whether people have knowledge. Can this contribute meaning to one's life? Is it *required* if your life is to be meaningful? Socrates claimed that the unexamined life is not worth living. Without a philosophical dimension, is one's life too shallow to be meaningful?

Yet we might wonder whether philosophical thinking *per se* is more meaningful than many other activities. Maybe it depends on *how* one is being philosophical – such as what one reflects on and how this affects what kind of person one is. In recent years, for example, there has emerged what is apparently a new way of trying to make people's lives more meaningful by making them more philosophical. It is generally called philosophical counselling. (I do not know how effective it is; I mention it only as an interesting idea.) A philosophical therapist listens to a patient's description of what is perplexing him or her about the world and about how to live. And sometimes it seems clear that the patient's underlying problem is philosophical, not psychological. For instance, the patient might not know whether what he or she is feeling is really love, and whether he or she is loved in turn. What is love? What is knowledge? (What is knowledge of one's own mind? What is knowledge of another's mind?) These are philosophical questions about reality and knowledge. A counsellor could ascertain what philosophical opinions the patient already has on these issues, before introducing him or her to pieces of philosophy with which to clarify and extend those opinions. This could even reveal What To Do. The point of thinking carefully is not simply to become more articulate. Rather, it is to increase the accuracy and depth in one's conception of the world and one's place in it – so much so as to gain knowledge with which to act wisely and well.

Of course, a meaningful life might not be comfortable. If you seek meaning through living philosophically, you must be open to the possibility of changing your opinions, even cherished ones. Any counsellors (like any philosophy teachers) who never confront you with the possibility of your personally important views being false are less-than-fully philosophical in their interactions with you. Might even sup-posedly philosophical counselling not provide meaning, if it merely comforts or satisfies, just reinforcing pre-existing views?

Question 4.6   Are all older people wiser and more knowledgeable than all younger people? ('You must respect your grandfather. He is so wise, having lived so long.') Or can older people be closed-minded-young-people-grown-older? Have such older people never had meaningful lives? Are all younger people more open-minded and imaginative than all older ones? ('We need more young faces around here. They'll bring new ideas, fresh thinking.') Or can younger people be closed-minded-old-people-in-waiting – ignorant, unreflective, conventional? Will such younger people never have meaningful lives?

Aristotle on the best way to live

We ask about the meaning of life. Then we struggle to understand our question, let alone to answer it. Can the great Greek philosopher Aristotle (384–322 BC) help us? In his *Nicomachean Ethics*, he asked a similar question: What is the best possible way in which a person could live? His discussion became one of the most influential in the history of philosophy; the following remarks capture a few of his views.

Often we speak about whether life has a point. Could the point of your life in particular be for you to manifest, via your specific proper-ties, whatever the point is of human life in general? And what is the lat-ter point? Why should there be one at all? Aristotle thought that of course there is a point – a goal, an end, an aim – to human life. It is whatever would be the most excellent way to be a person. It is whatever would be the ultimate or supreme good that there could be in living as a person. It could never be a means to some further good; for then it would not be the ultimate end.

Could accumulating financial wealth, for example, be part of that final aim? No, because in a balanced person money is only a means, not an end. Money is an arbitrary invention. It is not an aspect of what it is to be a person as such. The best possible end around which to structure one's life, argues Aristotle, is a certain form of happiness or flourishing. (His word for it was *eudaimonia*.) This is not simply a subjectively experi-enced state of pleasure. It is an actively flourishing life. Each of us aims at this, even if not always consciously. We do so insofar as we function as persons. (Actually, Aristotle talks of human beings, not persons. But more recent philosophers, as Chapter 1 explained, have asked whether being a human being is the same as being a person. In case it is not, I will continue talking of persons.)

What form does such flourishing take? Aristotle contends that, as persons, we can aim no higher than to act in accord with both virtue and intellect. Moral and intellectual virtues, practical and intellectual wisdom: no other animal is capable of these; so, we must strive to live by manifesting these ourselves (even as we do so among other people for whom this is no less essential). There is no guarantee that we can achieve this kind of life. But there is no higher goal to which a person – considered as a person, not simply as an animal – could aspire. To aim only for 'good times' with friends, eating, drinking, and passively watching one spectacle after another, falls well short of that. It is not to be meaningfully a person. Many kinds of animal could 'achieve' that much in their lives.

Aristotle thus brings together some themes we have encountered in this chapter. He tells us that the purpose of people's lives must be something available only to us (not other animals), that we are social beings, that the good life is ethical (manifesting various virtues), and that the good life is therefore contemplative, even philosophical. Only that is an ultimately good life; and only an ultimately good life is what a life should be. We usually use the phrase 'the good life' superficially, referring to those passing pleasures that constitute a less-than-ultimately good life. Aristotle describes for us a deeper good life – a life as only a person could live it, indeed as only a meaningful person could live it.

Aristotle's first step towards that conclusion is quite contentious, though. Is there really an inherent goal in living as a person – as against living just as something living? Aristotle's is a teleological theory (the Greek word *telos* means 'end'), because it is about the purpose he thinks there is in being a person. People who believe that there is a God often talk teleologically of there therefore being an end or purpose to personal existence. But what if their belief in God's existing is false? Then seemingly they would be as badly misled as those inhabitants of Plato's cave. There is that risk in making our sense of life's point or meaning depend on the belief that there is a God. (More generally, should we look to beliefs that are *clearly* true?)

'If we do not believe that there is a God, though, mustn't we refrain – depressingly – from claiming that there is a purpose or point to being a person?' The answer is not obvious. Maybe the following claims are available as an alternative (and Aristotelian) way of supporting the idea that there can be a purpose in being a person:

Some people live in more highly developed ways. These need not be conventionally or socially refined ways. They would be ways that make greater use of whatever properties are uniquely and enviably part of being a person. Perhaps these ways would not be the performing of great physical feats; other animals can do this. Maybe – for the same reason – those ways would not be one's socialising or 'preening' or 'looking good'. Possibly, what would constitute developed ways of being that are distinctive of persons are characteristics that involve having greater moral awareness and goodness, greater intellectual awareness and goodness.

Would people who are developed in such ways be better people – better as people? That is, would they be better examples of the very best of which a person in particular is capable – as against another kind of animal, or even a mere human being who fails to be a person (if there are human beings like that)?

However, would only such morally and intellectually well-developed people also have *meaningful* lives? Or can uneducated and unreflective people live meaningfully, for instance, so long as they are morally good and sensitive? Some people who are intelligent and thoughtful (even about morality) are uncaring and cruel; are their lives thereby meaningless? Admittedly, it could be difficult – without being somewhat arrogant and uncaring oneself – to dismiss a particular life as meaningless. But must we do so if we are to laud others, in contrast, as meaningful?

Of course, there is the possibility that no lives are ever either meaningful or meaningless (regardless of our saying that they are). Yet even if there are no meaningful or meaningless lives as such, is it still possible for there to be better or worse lives (in the Aristotelian sense described just now), and thus better or worse people? We could imagine Aristotle asking this; we should ask it ourselves.

Further reading

On life's meaningfulness in general:
> Oswald Hanfling (ed.), *Life and Meaning: A Reader* (Oxford: Blackwell, 1987).
>
> E.D. Klemke (ed.), *The Meaning of Life*, 2nd edn (New York: Oxford University Press, 2000).
>
> Robert Nozick, *Philosophical Explanations* (Cambridge, MA: Harvard University Press, 1981), pp. 571–9, 585–619.
>
> Jonathan Westphal and Carl Levenson (eds), *Life and Death* (Indianapolis, IN: Hackett, 1993).

On the myth of Sisyphus:
> Albert Camus, *The Myth of Sisyphus and Other Essays*, transl. Justin O'Brien (New York: Vintage, 1955).
>
> Richard Taylor, *Metaphysics*, 4th edn (Englewood Cliffs, NJ: Prentice-Hall, 1992), ch. 13.
>
> Richard Taylor, *Good and Evil* (Amherst, NY: Prometheus Books, 2000 [1970]), ch. 18.

For Plato's parable of the cave:
  Plato, *Republic* 514a–520d.

For Nozick's machines:
  Robert Nozick, *Anarchy, State, and Utopia* (New York: Basic Books, 1974), pp. 42–5.

On meaningfulness in living ethically:
  Peter Singer, *How are we to Live?: Ethics in an Age of Self-Interest* (Melbourne: Text Publishing, 1993), ch. 10.

On philosophical counselling:
  Lou Marinoff, *Plato, Not Prozac!: Applying Philosophy to Everyday Problems* (New York: HarperCollins, 1999).

For Aristotle's theory of the right way to live:
  Aristotle, *Nicomachean Ethics*, Bk I, and Bk X, chs 7, 8.

5

Death's Harm

Objective harm?

There will come a time when I am dead, when you are dead. We get no choice in this. Should we be emotionally overwhelmed by that fact? Should we fear death? We know that there are horrible ways to die: pain, degradation, and despair can characterise people's final years, days, moments. But not everyone dies like that. For many, death arrives swiftly, painlessly, during sleep. Should that sort of death be a dire prospect? Can it be bad to die even when no overt suffering is involved? This chapter focusses on these questions.

They are often discussed in religious terms. For example, many think that there is no harm in dying, because their religion assures them that there is an after-life or that each person's soul will be reincarnated: 'Do I dread death? No. God will tend to my soul – which is, of course, me.'

But our questions about death are not inherently religious. They are metaphysical. And although various religions proffer metaphysical answers to those questions, those religions' answers might be false. The claim that each person has a non-physical soul is hardly self-evidently true (as we saw in Chapter 1 (Dualism)). Nor, therefore, is the claim that a person can enjoy an after-life, courtesy of his or her non-physical soul's continued survival. The claim, too, that there is a God is no less metaphysical – and no less open to being philosophically questioned (as Chapter 3 demonstrated). Neither a view's being religious, nor its being comforting, is a good indicator of its being true. (And if it is not true, it is not an insight.) In practice, this means that when philosophers try to answer questions about life and death, they do not presuppose religious answers. In a philosophical context, religions must be argued for, as must any competing theories.

Accordingly, here is this chapter's main question:

Can death be bad for one who dies (assuming that no after-life or reincarnation awaits him or her), even when this involves no felt suffering by him or her?

That question concerns the possibility of death's being *objectively* harmful for the person who dies. You are not harmed by your death just because you feel bad (if you do) when thinking about your future death. That feeling is real, and perhaps it is harmful. ('I find the whole idea frightening. Surely I'm harmed by feeling that way.') But that harm is being done to your life by how you are living that life – by living with that feeling. It is not thereby done to your life by your no longer living. Moreover, is it possible that your feeling is mistaken? If it is mistaken, yet you retain it, then you are harmed only by your mistaken feeling that your death will harm you. You would be making your life bleaker than it need be, by dreading what would not merit dread.

Of course, to note this is not to show that such a feeling is misleading. It is to remark only that such a mistake is possible. We need to examine whether people are ever really harmed by their deaths – or whether they merely think that they will be.

Question 5.1   Is a dead body still a person? Although we often refer to dead bodies as if they are still persons ('Look at Arnold over there. He's dead.'), *should* we do so? For how long, if at all, after dying might a person continue to exist as that person? Ten seconds? Ten minutes? Ten days? Ten years? Is a decaying body a decaying person? Should we respect a dead body (and not abuse it) only in the way that we respect (and do not abuse) an admired sculpture, say?

Epicurus and Lucretius on being dead

Whether death is harmful depends upon what death involves. Let's distinguish, for a start, between *being dead* and *dying*. In this section and the next, we consider whether your being dead could harm you; then the section, Dying, will be about whether your dying – painlessly – could do so.

We begin by perusing some classic arguments from ancient Greece – specifically, from Epicurus (c. 341–270 BC) and Lucretius (c. 99–55 BC). Epicurus was a popular philosopher for many years; Lucretius was strongly influenced by him. Only fragments of Epicurus's writings have survived. These include the following argument for its being impossible – yes, impossible – to be harmed by being dead. Epicurus claimed that there is a metaphysical incompatibility between incurring harm and being dead.

Pivotal to his reasoning for that conclusion was a thesis to this effect:

Being harmed involves having awkward or unpleasant experiences. To be harmed is to suffer.

If we accept that thesis (thought Epicurus), we must infer that no one could be harmed once dead. Epicurus assumed (and most philosophers still agree) that once a person is dead, he or she cannot have experiences – the ability to have them being a sure sign of not being dead! But then it follows (concluded Epicurus) that being dead cannot harm the person who has died. Here is the relevant reasoning:

If you are harmed, you suffer. If you suffer, you are alive. If you are dead, you are not alive. So, if you are dead, you are not harmed.

Lucretius accepted that Epicurean reasoning. He also proposed a further argument for the impossibility of being harmed by being dead. He took it that any harm there could be in one's being dead is due to one's not being alive. But before you were born, you were also not alive. You were not alive in 1800, just as you will not be alive in 2200. Yet clearly, Lucretius would say, you were not harmed by not being alive in 1800 – prior to being born. It is equally clear, therefore, that you will not be harmed by not being alive in 2200 – when you are dead. Because non-existence prior to being alive is not harmful, neither is non-existence after having been alive (infers Lucretius).

Epicurus and Lucretius share the conviction that it is irrational to be frightened of being dead. It is irrational (in their view), for this reason:

One would be fearing a supposed harm in being dead. But it is metaphysically confused to think that there is ever any such harm. And this confusion is easy to correct (via the simple Epicurean and Lucretian reasoning, outlined in this section).

To which you might respond in these terms:

Correcting that confusion is more easily advocated than achieved. Although I can intellectually appreciate the force in the reasoning by Epicurus and Lucretius, I cannot live in accord with it. For they are being cavalier about life. Would they urge us not to care about our lives right now (given their believing that there is no possible harm for us in being dead)?

Epicurus and Lucretius would definitely not offer that advice. The Epicurean ideal was to live well and wisely, appreciating that only life can give pleasure. Do not think that being dead will be either a boon or a bane (Epicurus would have urged). Make the most of life while you have it. Do not be scared by the fact that there will come a time when you are dead. By having that fear, you simply lessen your pleasure in life, right here, right now. And that harms you, even as being dead cannot.

Question 5.2   Suppose that you wish to compete in a race scheduled for next year. But suppose also that by the time the race occurs, you will be dead. Are you therefore harmed already, by desiring to do what – as it happens – you will be unable to do? Is your life unwittingly somewhat pointless because of this? ('If she had only realised that she was soon to die, she would have directed her energies elsewhere – not towards competing in that race. It's a pity that she was engaged in what – as we realised later – was pointless preparation.')

Being deprived by being dead?

Contemporary philosophers tend to think that Epicurus and Lucretius, in reasoning as they did, relied upon too narrow a conception of harm. The Epicurean conception says that to be harmed is to suffer a bad experience. And this thinking leads naturally to the Epicurean conclusion that there is no harm in being dead – because once you are dead, you have no experiences at all, including bad ones. Nonetheless, might there be ways of being harmed that do not involve having bad experiences? Perhaps you could be harmed less directly than by having an unpleasant experience. Possibly, there are ways to be harmed 'silently' – unknowingly, painlessly. Could being dead harm you in some such way?

What would 'silent' – unexperienced – harm be like? Some philosophers believe that it could be one's being unwittingly *deprived* of opportunities. The idea is that you could be harmed in that way without ever having associated bad experiences. Instead, you would simply miss out on what would have been associated good experiences. Does that occur when, for example, people are victims of hidden yet odiously discriminatory behaviour? They might be harmed by being overlooked for various jobs, while never knowing of the covert prejudices preventing their being hired.

Could a person's being dead harm him or her in that way? Is it possible that being dead will deny you opportunities that would otherwise have been open to you? What is usually called the *deprivation analysis* says that you could be harmed in that way by being dead. For example, if – were it not for being dead – you would have had more good experiences than bad, then you are harmed by their being rendered unavailable to you, due to your being dead. ('He's dead. Now he'll never climb Mt Everest; he so wanted to do that! Poor guy.') Clearly, many people regard a person's being dead as depriving him or her of opportunities. If this reaction is even occasionally accurate, then being dead can be harmful (regardless of whether other people are not harmed by being dead). And Epicurus would be wrong, having denied that being dead *ever* harms one.

The deprivation analysis could well be regarded as being a commonsense sort of theory. Nevertheless, does it succumb to the following objections?

An Epicurean objection   The deprivation analysis misunderstands the nature of deprivation. Being deprived of something includes having some experiences instead of others (which one would probably have appreciated). Part of being deprived of a job (due to prejudice, say) is one's not subsequently having experiences of doing that job. However, it is also, in part, one's having alternative experiences, either of performing a different job or of being unemployed (perhaps still seeking a job). Hence, if having alternative experiences is part of what it is to be deprived of something, then being dead is not a deprivation. For in being dead one has no alternative experiences. This argument is Epicurean in spirit, because it conceives of deprivation as a matter, in part, of what experiences we have: we fail to have some specific experiences (maybe ones we really desired); we have alternative ones. And the moral of this argument against the deprivation analysis is simple: Although, by being dead, one *does not have* various possible experiences, one is not thereby *deprived* of them.

A Lucretian objection   If (as the deprivation analysis asserts) you are deprived of opportunities once you are dead, then surely (we may equally well assert, in a Lucretian spirit) you were deprived of opportunities until you were alive. Yet the latter would be an absurd way to talk. Until you exist, there is no *you* to be deprived of anything. By analogy, therefore, there is no you being deprived of anything once you are dead. 'No, look at Arnold there, dead,' you might object, 'he is being deprived of ... oh, so much that he could have been enjoying.' But Arnold will be dead for a long, long time – forever more, in fact. Will he be deprived of opportunities throughout that whole period? Having been dead for two seconds, is Arnold already being deprived of opportunities? Having been dead for two weeks, is he still being deprived of opportunities? Having been dead for two months, or two years, or two decades, or two centuries, and so on, does he continue being deprived of opportunities? It sounds less and less plausible to claim that such deprivation is occurring, the longer that Arnold has been dead. However, at no single one of those many moments is he more dead than at any other one of them. Accordingly, we should infer that at none of those moments is Arnold being deprived by being dead. He is not being deprived even two seconds after having died.

Question 5.3   Are you dying at each moment when you are living? When dying, one is living; when living, is one dying? Later on in one's living, does the process of one's dying just become more apparent? (It has always been irreversible, hasn't it?) Are more or less pleasant lives just more or less pleasant ways to be dying?

Dying

Even if being dead cannot be bad for you, might you be harmed by dying? Dying and being dead are metaphysically distinct. Whereas being dead is a state, dying is an event or process. And your dying occurs within your life: you might consciously experience your dying; you at least undergo it, maybe unconsciously. When people reflect on the prospect of death, often it seems that they have in mind their dying. So, let's ask whether you can be harmed by dying (even if not by subsequently being dead).

The arguments of Epicurus and Lucretius do not address that question. They concern your being dead, hence your being unable to have experiences at that time. In contrast, your dying can be experienced by you. And obviously it could harm you by being a painful experience. That is not the philosophically difficult case to consider, though. Our question (in the section, Objective harm?) was whether death can be harmful even when not painful. Many people fear not only whatever pain might be experienced when dying; they fear the dying as such. Even a painless death strikes many as an awful prospect. They apparently think of dying as being a special harm – so that a person would be harmed even by an instantaneous and painless death that gives no prior indication of being imminent. Even if there is no harm for that person in having died – in being dead – could there be harm in undergoing this painless and immediate and unannounced dying?

Here are a few suggestions that might be offered in support of the claim that one's dying can harm one (along with possible responses to the suggestions).

Opportunity deprivation   'My dying will deprive me of opportunities.' But that is not enough to make dying harmful. Most substantive events within your life cut off various opportunities; we do not therefore classify them as harming you. 'Yes, but those other events can create different opportunities, often better ones: by losing one job, I might gain a better one. Dying cannot do that.' Even so, dying is not thereby deprivational. Dying deprives you of opportunities only insofar as your being dead will do so; yet we have seen (in the section, Being deprived by being dead?) how unclear it is that being dead deprives you of opportunities.

Experience cessation 'My dying will bring to an end those experiences that enrich my life, such as moments of pleasure. I enjoy my life; dying will end it.' However, would you actually be harmed by having your experiences ended? ('My opportunities for continued pleasure would be lost.' Again, though, are you really being *deprived* of further opportunities for pleasure?) Are continued experiences so vital anyway? Is there some appropriate amount of pleasure in a life, for example, with anything less than that leaving one short of what one is 'owed' as a person? You might want your experiences to continue; yet you are not *harmed* simply because the good times are ending. You always knew that they would do so sometime. And perhaps their point was to enrich your life – without thereby having any further point. Once the life ends, they end. So too, therefore, does there being any point to their not ending. (But note that this reasoning would not show that being plunged suddenly into an irreversible coma is not harmful. After all, in that situation, the life has not ended, even though the experiences have.)

So far, then, we might be struggling to understand how a person's dying painlessly and unwittingly could harm his or her life. Is the following suggestion any more helpful?

Meaninglessness 'My dying renders *futile* my hopes for my future beyond (as it happens) the time when I will die.' Suppose that (as the sections, Epicurus and Lucretius on being dead, and Being deprived by being dead?, suggested) your being dead cannot harm you. If you are nevertheless hurt by dying, this harm is present as part of how you are living your life (as against being a consequence eventuating only once you are dead). It is not uncommon for people to suspect that the certainty of dying casts a pall of pointlessness over living. That could sound like a needlessly strong reaction. Still, maybe the certainty of dying undermines many of our hopes for the future; and this might harm us.

Here is how that could occur. We encountered (in Chapter 4, Nozick's machines) the possibility of one's life becoming *meaningless* once one either does or should lose hope. And perhaps whatever makes one's life meaningless in that way and for that time thereby harms one's life, at least for that while. Could dying make one's life meaningless in that way? (Could 'giving up' on life even while living it do likewise?) Once you are dying, whatever hopes you have for your life beyond any time at which you are still dying can no longer be fulfilled. Hence, if you are aware of dying, those hopes will or should disappear. And if you are unaware of dying (for instance, if you die while asleep), then any hopes you still have at that time for your future actions are, as it has turned out, objectively futile – even though you need not be aware of this. In one way or another, therefore, will your dying make your life objectively meaningless while the dying is occurring? Can your dying – regardless of how painless it might be – thereby harm your life during that time? (And is dying young more likely to be harmful in this way, insofar as younger people generally have more hopes for the future than do old people, at any rate?)

This prompts a disturbing thought. Maybe (it might be said) you should never live 'for the future' by *having* hopes: you should live 'only for the present moment'. (You never know for sure that you are not about to die. So, you never know for sure that your life is not meaningless right now, due to including desires which are about to be rendered futile by your dying.) However, even if it is possible to live like that (without desires for the future), would doing so be another way to make your life meaningless? Would it be a kind of 'living death', effectively being 'dead' before one has died? That would be ironic, because people often think of living 'for the present moment' as intensifying one's living – as being more alive, so to speak. Yet is a life *already* harmed if it contains no desires for the future?

Question 5.4   Imagine an injury leaving you in a coma, with only this thought running through your mind, over and over: 'I'm alive. That's good.' Would death be better for you than living the rest of your life in that way (being kept alive on machinery in a hospital)? Or is being alive of paramount value, regardless of how experientially impoverished it is? (How little experience can an ongoing life contain?)

Never dying

If you believe that dying will be bad, no matter how painless, should you also believe that it would be better never to die? You might think that, insofar as you will be harmed by dying as such, you would be less harmed, overall, if you could avoid dying. In other words, you might believe that a kind of immortality would be preferable – the kind whereby, once born, you live eternally. Is dying so bad as to render everlasting living good?

At present, we have no realistic idea of how a person could live forevermore. Probably, it will never be possible. But our question right now is whether such an outcome would be good if possible, not whether it is possible. Is it worth seeking? Should we yearn for it, saddened by its present unavailability?

It is tempting to think, 'I wish I could live forever.' The reality might fall far short of the fantasy, though. There is no way to guarantee living eternally at one's physical and mental peak. Indeed, to suppose that one's prolonged existence would be like that is to deny – surely in a spirit of fantasy – that the ageing and decline we already undergo would occur at all. (And would that be *us*? Would those creatures even be people?)

Might we suppose, alternatively, that eternal life would include our ageing as we do, but much more slowly? In that case, eternal life would seemingly be awful for many people – more awful than life as they already know it. There is no way to guarantee that one's eternally extended life would not contain infinite – and currently unlived – misery. If there is no way for you to know in advance that your undying life would not be like that, should the idea of living eternally be as scary for you as the prospect of dying is to many people now? Perhaps eternal life is therefore not obviously superior to a life that ends with one's dying. (Remember, too, that even an eternal life could be meaningless. In Chapter 4, The myth of Sisyphus, Sisyphus's was apparently like that.)

You might be confident that a wholly good God would sustain your everlasting survival, perhaps in a disembodied form, certainly in a blessed and enviable state. But again (as the section, Objective harm?, noted), two earlier chapters reveal how sternly philosophers question the key elements of that comforting story. From Chapter 3, it is not philosophically clear whether there is a wholly good God. And from Chapter 1, it is not philosophically clear whether a disembodied entity would really be you.

In any event, why should eternal disembodied existence be desirable? There might well be no guarantee that you would continue to live, in a disembodied way, at your mental and emotional peak. And possibly those disembodied beings would become overwhelmingly bored by unending existence. Either there would not be enough for them to do mentally (after a long while, they might have exhausted their mental capacities). Or maybe they were never notably mentally active people in the first place (a purely mental existence could be far from what they desire). Unending boredom: There is a hint of Sisyphus in this situation.

Question 5.5   If no one were ever to die, would this affect the nature of morality? For instance, would attempted murder be no more immoral than assault – bad, but not as much so as we now assume it to be? If only some people were never to die, would this give them a moral superiority over others? If so, are all older people morally superior, other things being equal, to all younger people? Or is longevity as such irrelevant to a life's moral worth?

Brain death

If the harm incurred by dying painlessly (if there is any such harm) is not so bad as to make everlasting life preferable, then does the *quality* of one's life matter more, at least sometimes, than the fact of one's living? Doctors face this question in practice, since it is they who legally determine whether a person is dying or dead, and because often they must balance, on the one hand, whether a person can be kept alive and, on the other hand, whether keeping the person alive would give him or her a life worth living. We are all familiar in principle with this partly ethical issue. But might some such mental balancing act enter the medical process even earlier? Is it possible that the medical determination of a person as being dead in the first place is already partly ethical? Or do doctors, when determining such matters, respond only to physical – scientifically describable – aspects of the person in front of them? These questions are prompted by the following considerations.

The ultimate bodily criterion used by doctors in establishing that a person has died is the person's brain's having ceased to function. This is called brain death. It takes two main forms. A brain might stop functioning altogether; or those parts of it that sustain consciousness could do so. Each of these two bodily signs has been used by doctors. And is this in itself worrying – the fact that two slightly different criteria of death have been applied to people? If only one of these two criteria is correct, quite possibly people have been classified as dead who were not really dead! If we apply the consciousness criterion, yet in fact a person is alive if there is even some brain activity, then someone's brain could be classified as being dead (because he or she will never regain consciousness) – even while other activity in his or her brain actually suffices for its not being dead.

Is it possible, too, that brain death is not really the death of the person? Is this possible, even if people are purely physical beings? After all, a person could be brain dead while some other internal organs are functioning, such as his or her heart and lungs. And might a person not really be dead, so long as these continue functioning?

I do not know whether a person would be alive in that situation. But that question arises because of how the brain death criterion was derived. The criterion emanates from a 1968 report by what became known as the Harvard Brain Death Committee. The committee sought a new standard for death – one that made more functioning organs available for use in transplant operations. Unless a person is officially deemed to be dead, his or her organs cannot legally be removed, even to save another person's life. And how could a person reasonably be deemed dead if his or her heart is still pumping blood, say? The Harvard committee's suggestion was simple: Brain death suffices for being dead. So – and how fortuitous this was – a person can be dead, according to this criterion, even while some of his or her other organs are functioning sufficiently well to be transplanted to someone else. With almost every country having since adopted the brain death criterion, therefore, some people may now legally be classified as dead, who would previously have been said to be alive; and other people's lives can now be saved by transplantations that became legally possible upon the adoption of this new criterion of death.

The new criterion might be more accurate than any earlier criterion. It might even be completely correct. But there is a philosophical question as to *what sort of fact* doctors now know, in knowing that a person is dead-because-brain-dead. Is it a purely physical fact? Is it a partly ethical fact? Most people, as far as I can tell, assume that a doctor, in determining a person's being dead-because-brain-dead, is discovering a purely physical fact about that person. Yet that medical determination might also reflect, ultimately, some ethical (and perhaps praiseworthy) motivations on the part of many doctors – particularly a desire to save other people's lives, when the quality of a given person's life has deteriorated wholly and irretrievably. Have decisions to amend the official medical criterion of death reflected interests other than the narrowly scientific one of being as accurate and certain as possible about whether a person is dead?

Thus, in thinking about the metaphysics of death, we face this question:

Is death always a purely physical feature of the person who dies?

When ascertaining whether a person is dead, will doctors only need evidence of his or her physical state? Or will they, at least occasionally, also require some philosophical understanding of the situation's ethical ramifications? Which aspects of the world make true our beliefs that various people are dead? (This depends, in part, upon the nature of truth – which is the subject of Chapter 7.)

Further reading

On death in general:

Fred Feldman, *Confrontations with the Reaper: A Philosophical Study of the Nature and Value of Death* (New York: Oxford University Press, 1992).

John Martin Fischer (ed.), *The Metaphysics of Death* (Stanford, CA: Stanford University Press, 1993).

Jeff McMahan, *The Ethics of Killing: Problems at the Margins of Life* (New York: Oxford University Press, 2002), ch. 2.

Thomas Nagel, *The View from Nowhere* (New York: Oxford University Press, 1986), pp. 223–31.

Robert Nozick, *Philosophical Explanations* (Cambridge, MA: Harvard University Press, 1981), pp. 579–85.

For Epicurus and Lucretius on being dead:
A.A. Long and D.N. Sedley (eds & trans.), *The Hellenistic Philosophers*, vol. 1 (Cambridge: Cambridge University Press, 1987), pp. 149–54.

On the deprivation analysis:
Thomas Nagel, *Mortal Questions* (Cambridge: Cambridge University Press, 1979), ch. 1.

On immortality:
D.Z. Phillips, *Death and Immortality* (London: Macmillan, 1970), ch. 1.
Bernard Williams, *Problems of the Self: Philosophical Papers 1956–1972* (Cambridge: Cambridge University Press, 1973), ch. 6.

On brain death and life's quality:
Jonathan Glover, *Causing Death and Saving Lives* (London: Penguin, 1990 [1977]), pp. 43–57.
Peter Singer, *Rethinking Life and Death: The Collapse of our Traditional Ethics* (New York: St Martin's Press, 1994), ch. 2.

6

Properties

The problem of universals

The world has structure – constituents, aspects, parts. It includes you; does it thereby include your properties? In earlier chapters, we have been especially concerned with ascertaining some of our fundamental properties – trying to formulate a correct metaphysics of what it is to be whatever we are. For example, are you just physical, yet with a free will and bearing moral responsibility for your actions? You do not think of either yourself or the rest of the world as a featureless blob. Instead, you attribute properties – features, characteristics – both to yourself and to much else. In this way, you paint a picture of reality. You observe and think, seeking to understand yourself and the world, by knowing what properties are possessed by you or other parts of reality. You aim to know what you and the world are *like*.

Philosophers have long wondered what it is for something to have a property. We talk glibly of something's being thus-and-so, having a specific characteristic, possessing some feature. But what do such claims mean? And what does it mean to say that two things *share* a property? What is it for you and I to share the property of being a person? Such questions plunge us into *the problem of universals*. This intellectual challenge has been part of philosophy for as long as philosophy has been part of humanity. The challenge is still with us, because there is no philosophical consensus on how to solve it. Here is one way in which it can arise.

For argument's sake, suppose that physicalism (introduced in Chapter 1, Physicalism) is true of the whole world. Then you and I, like everything else, are instances of physical stuff – nothing more, nothing less. We are organisations of particles, say (for simplicity). Accordingly, right now the world contains a you-collection and a me-collection. These are distinct collections, sharing not even one particle right now.

You are your collection; I am mine. In this way, we are fundamentally distinct beings.

Yet are we really so distinct? After all, each of us is a person. Each of us has skin, speaks and reads at least one language, has been alive for several years, and so on. We seem to have properties in common. We say that we do; and we seem to be literally correct about that. Although I have my hair and you have yours (with yours being over there, wholly distinct from mine, over here), we share the property of having hair. Similarly, even as we are different people, we are one – in the sense of sharing the property of being a person. (As the chorus of an Australian song goes: 'I am, you are, we are Australian.') Indeed, don't we share many properties? Don't we have much in common – literally?

But the two previous paragraphs clash with each other. To accept both is to accept these conclusions:

1. *Not sharing*   You and I are fundamentally distinct, with nothing literally in common.
2. *Sharing*   You and I literally have much in common.

And 1 and 2 cannot both be true, even if so far each has seemed true. How can this clash be resolved? If it cannot, do we fail to understand how two individuals could share a characteristic?

The clash is dramatic. For here is an alternative version of 1:

You and I do not literally have any properties in common.

And that remarkable claim implies this one:

If I am a person, you are not. If I have hair, you do not. And so on, for any property: If I have it, you do not.

Even this is implied:

If I am a person, no one else is a person. If I have hair, no one else has hair. And so on, for any property: If I have it, no one else does.

So, 1's clash with 2 could not be more stark. Two people not sharing all properties prevents them from sharing even one: because of our differences, we have literally nothing in common.

But our everyday ways of thinking and speaking tell us otherwise. Although we acknowledge differences between individuals, we also – unavoidably – use words that suggest generality, such as 'person'. We apply those words to more than one thing. And this openness to the prospect of properties being shared – to distinct individual things having features in common – is why the problem of universals has the name it does. You apply a word such as 'person' to a single individual, while presuming that in theory the word could apply to other individuals, too – that more than one person might exist. However, if 1 and 2 are correct, that view of the world has to go. Again, therefore, do we not understand how there can be many individuals sharing a feature? And if so, do we fail to comprehend how even a single individual has some feature? That would be disastrous for our knowing what the world is like. We are left, then, with the problem of universals looming much larger than we probably anticipated. In the next five sections, I outline some of the many ways in which philosophers have sought to solve that problem.

Question 6.1   'It's what I do. It's not what I am,' I once heard (on TV) a famous 'supermodel' say about her modelling. Yet how far can such a distinction be taken? Aren't your actions still aspects of you – properties of yours? Are they therefore part of you, helping to make you whatever you are? Are they part of you, at least, if you perform them day after day, year after year?

Platonic Forms

Could it be that we need to look beyond the world of particles – the physical world – in analysing how an individual has a property? Plato would have said so. His has been the most historically significant attempt to solve the problem of universals. (He also helped to pose the problem in the first place.) His basic idea (when applied to you and me) would say that each of us is a human being because of the relationship each of us bears to some non-physical entity outside this observable, physical world. That special entity is what Plato called the Form of being a human being. (Modern adaptations of Plato's theory would also talk of the Form of being a person – as I will often do in this section.) A Form is a non-physical universal. It is an abstract ideal. It is eternal, unchangeable. You and I grow, change, and decay as persons; the Form of Person does not.

It is not entirely clear what further characteristics Plato took Forms to have. What is clear, though, is that the world of Plato's Forms was not restricted to the Form of Human Being. Plato argued that there are many Forms. (You should also be aware that translations of Plato's writings sometimes use the word 'Idea' rather than 'Form'. To us, however, that suggests something existing just mentally – which is not how Forms were conceived of by Plato.) In general, when two individual things in this world are alike in some respect, Plato thought of this as requiring the existence of an independent Form. He was not sure whether there is a Form for every property we seem to observe; would there be a Form corresponding to something's being a filthy puddle of mud? But Forms help to give the world its features much of the time, thought Plato. Two dogs are dogs because the Form of Dog exists. Two cats are cats because the Form of Cat exists. Most importantly, there are such Forms as those of Truth, Beauty, and Goodness. The Forms, for Plato, were metaphysically – and even ethically – special.

It is therefore particularly pressing to understand how a Form could apply to individuals like us, as we muddle about in our spatio-temporal world. Does the Form of Person apply to you because you are *like* it, resembling it? How could that be so? The Form of Person, unlike you, is not changeable, mutable. Is the Form of Person instead a perfect or ideal person? Or is it a paradigm – a standard or fully representative – person? It is tempting to conceive of Forms along such lines. But can we ever understand what either a perfect or a paradigm person would be like? And surely the Form of Person could not be an imperfect person, either. Such a Form would not be eternal, immutable, an ideal standing equally well to everyone (even taking into account the vast array of variations among individual persons). Is the Form of Person thus not a person, or even like a person? Is it a perfect … non-person? If so, then how could it be a Form of Person, rather than of something else – a Form for some kind of Almost-Person?

Plato formulated no full theory of Forms. His discussions were exploratory and fascinatingly suggestive. He even acknowledged the difficulty of knowing that Forms exist. They are not part of this spatio-temporal world, the world we perceive; if we are to know of them, it must be through pure reflection. Your senses tell you that there is a dog in front of you, but they do not reveal the Form of Dog. Pure thought would be needed for that; and pure thought is not trivially available (if it is available at all, something we will contemplate in Chapter 11). Platonic Realism is the usual name for any theory (such as Plato's own version) according to which there are eternal Forms, without which nothing in this world would have particular features.

Aristotle, for one, thought that Plato's theory made universals needlessly mysterious. For Plato, Forms would exist even if we and other spatio-temporal particulars were not to do so. But Aristotle thought that when universals exist, they do so by applying to actual things; and in doing this they are spatio-temporal themselves. If there were no persons, there would be no property of personhood (according to Aristotle); as it is, the property of personhood exists in space and time no less than we do.

Yet might a mystery persist, even in Aristotle's seemingly sensible way of thinking? How can personhood be wholly present in each of us, if it is as spatio-temporally located as we are? (How could it be a universal, not a particular – as you, I, and spatio-temporal locations are particular?) And if personhood is less than wholly present in each of us, perhaps because it is somehow 'scattered' throughout the world, then are we not really – because not fully – people?

Question 6.2   Is there a property of being evil? Is there one of being morally good? Are there properties of being cruel, being in pain, being in undeserved pain? Are there properties of being racist, being sexist, being a snob about money or social status? 'Of course there are such properties. Otherwise, we couldn't talk of them. We wouldn't have the words we have for them.' Might words only be *intended* to be about such properties, though? Might their availability deceive us into thinking that they describe real properties in the world? Do all general terms pick out real properties? Can we know what the world is like, simply by studying the words with which we try to describe the world?

Label nominalism

Talking of Platonic Forms can be beguiling. But few philosophers who seek to solve the problem of universals are Platonic Realists, it seems. Most reach for some sort of *nominalism* instead. Nominalists claim that nothing is repeatable, strictly speaking: nothing can exist wholly in two places at once. What seem to be repeatable properties – that is, what seem to be universals – are just particular things, perhaps arranged aptly. In this section and the next two, I introduce particular kinds of nominalism. Let's begin with what we might call *label* nominalism.

Label nominalism encompasses two traditional nominalisms – *linguistic* nominalism and *conceptualism*. According to linguistic nominalists, particular words make individuals what they are. According to conceptualists, it is particular mental concepts that do so. These nominalists claim that words or concepts – in short, *labels* – not only describe and categorise; they also create. You and I are persons because instances of the word 'person', for example, are consistently used of us (say linguistic nominalists). So, there is no need to posit transcendent Forms, existing eternally and immutably. Whether two individuals are dogs is a matter of how we talk and think: If we categorise them as dogs, then that is what they are. Moreover, it is *why* they are as they are. Language and thought are that metaphysically powerful (conclude label nominalists).

And here are two standard objections to any such nominalism.

Objectivity   It is far from clear that words and thoughts are that powerful. Not all reality is linguistic or mental. A dog is not a dog *because* it is described as being a dog (with some word like 'dog' being used of it). Presumably, you would still be a person even if no one had ever called you a person. Aren't you and I people because of features we have in ourselves – objectively? Although people are generally called 'people', this is not what makes them people. Maybe some properties are only present because we say that they are – such as the property of being a shop. (If no one ever regarded some particular establishment as being a shop, it would not be a shop.) But seemingly not all properties are like that. There is much to the world which we try to describe, and which we do not create by describing it as we do. We seek to ascertain the world's characteristics, its properties; we do not always create those features of it simply by talking or thinking.

Repeatable meanings   A label nominalist claims that you are a person because a word or concept, such as 'person', is consistently applied to you. But unless those uses have a shared meaning, they are merely distinct sounds or marks (like distinct particles) that sound or look alike. So, we assume that the different uses are instances of a repeatable word-type or concept-type, this being why they mean the same. There is a shared, repeatable, meaning – person. However, that assumption is not clearly possible for a label nominalist, for whom there cannot be repeatable – generic, abstract – word-types or thought-types. Are purported label nominalists therefore not genuine nominalists? In trying to make their suggestion sound plausible, they seem to be relying upon a covert Platonism about meanings – treating them as linguistic or mental repeatables, linguistic or mental universals. This undermines the supposed nominalist solution to the problem of universals.

Question 6.3   Was Hamlet a man? Was he Danish? Did he possess a memorable turn of phrase? In brief, did he have properties? We tend to say that he was an articulate Danish man. Yet we also concede that he did not really exist. Do we therefore have a metaphysically confused conception of Hamlet? How can something that does not exist have properties? (Is there a property of not existing – which some things(!) have? Does the purple toad on your head have it?) Or is Hamlet, along with his properties, created by various *words* that purportedly describe him? (If so, where is he right now?) Did Shakespeare literally create that articulate Danish man?

Class nominalism

Nominalists have often thought that objectivity can be attained, and repeatability avoided, by conceiving of properties as groups or classes of individuals. The property of being a person would simply be a group of particular things. It would be the class of exactly those things that happen to be persons. This analysis is thus a *class nominalism*. Properties would be particular groupings of the world's particular things. An individual could belong to many such groups, too. Just as you would be a person by belonging to the group of persons, you would be male, or you would be female, by belonging to another particular group – the class of all and only males, or the class of all and only females. This is all there is, according to class nominalism, in your having various properties.

Here is one worry about class nominalism, however: It makes the possession of a property so *fragile*. Consider the property of being a person. Right now, there is a particular number and distribution of people within the world. You are in that group, as am I. Yet if our sharing the property of being a person is simply our each belonging to that group (as class nominalism claims), what happens to us as persons if the group changes its membership? By definition, it would no longer be the same group. (A particular group is replaced by a new one whenever there is a change of members. Definitionally, classes are constituted by their members: if even one member leaves, a new class is the result.) Hence, if our being persons was our belonging to that group, we would no longer be people.

This is a realistic worry, because the group of the world's persons does change. It changes repeatedly: each minute, people die, and apparently new ones come into existence. Are you now not a person, due to the death of someone in Papua New Guinea ten seconds ago? 'Of course not.' Like it or not, though, that death has deprived you of the property of being a person – if (as class nominalism claims) your having that property eleven seconds ago was merely your belonging to what was then the class of the world's persons.

That would be a remarkable way to cease being a person – so much so that no one really believes that we would no longer be persons in that circumstance. But how can class nominalists consistently have that reaction to the case? They might reply like this:

> No, there was a group of persons eleven seconds ago and now there is a slightly different group of persons. These groups of individuals have something in common. This is what makes each of those individuals, including me, a person. I am a member of both classes of people – the earlier group and the later one – because I satisfy this further criterion.

However, that natural reply relinquishes the class nominalist idea that all there is to being a person is belonging to a particular group. It looks instead to some independent criterion of why a given individual is in the particular group – and is thereby a person. That reply is therefore unavailable to class nominalists.

Question 6.4   Could a famous painting be forged so flawlessly that the original and the copy are intrinsically indistinguishable? Suppose the two are swapped back and forth – until no one knows which is the original. Should each then be worth a lot of money? Should each be valueless? Or should each be worth some intermediate amount? Should a painting's value be due to its intrinsic properties (its composition, texture, and so on)? Should the value also be due, at least partly, to its extrinsic properties (such as having been painted by this person, not that one)? Which properties should be more important – the intrinsic ones? the extrinsic ones?

Resemblance nominalism

Many nominalists look to the relevant resemblances obtaining between individuals as being that which groups individuals together, giving them properties in common. This thought generates *resemblance* nominalism. According to this version of nominalism, what is common to people, for instance, is the fact that we resemble each other insofar as we are persons. We do not resemble non-persons similarly. Somehow, to some sufficient extent, each of us resembles each of us. This is what makes each of us a person.

But that is not a complete analysis. I resemble many horses in having brown hair; I resemble all giraffes in being taller than all poodles; I resemble some lions in having rather unkempt hair. Does this make me a horse or giraffe or lion? Of course not. Resembling in one respect does not always suffice for resembling in another respect. It is the *respects* in which one individual resembles another to which we must attend. Having said that, though, might there be no one particular respect in which each person resembles each other person? (Think of how much variation there is among people.) Might there be none, at least, other than the specific property of being a person? And to cite that property would hardly help the resemblance nominalist. At best, citing it would explain why, in being persons, we resemble each other. However, it would not explain why, in resembling each other, we are persons. It would presume that we already understand how we are persons, prior to pointing out facts about resemblance in order to explain why we are persons. Accordingly, it would make the attempted explanation pointless or redundant. It would not reveal that, because we resemble each other, we are thereby persons.

Moreover, if we do resemble each other in some respect which suffices for our being persons (such as that of having human DNA), it is that property's presence which makes each of us a person. It is not the sharing of it as such which does so. Once more, therefore, resemblance as such is not a sufficient explanation of how we are persons. Resemblance flows *from* what makes each of us a person; it does not explain why something makes each of us a person.

It is unsurprising that resemblance nominalism has that failing. For it implies that you are a person only if there is at least one other person – someone whom you resemble. It implies that a particular stone is a stone only if there is at least one other stone – one which it resembles. The world could not contain just one stone! Yet aren't some properties – including those of being a person and being a stone – present *intrinsically* when they are present? (Not all properties are like that. A shop is a shop, remember, in part because of how it is regarded within a social setting.) In other words, aren't the following propositions true?

> You are a person in yourself – regardless of whether you resemble others. (If you resemble them, this is a consequence of each of you being a person. It is not what makes each of you a person.)

> If there had only ever been one stone in the world, it would still have been a stone. That is, there could have been merely one stone in the world.

Resemblance nominalism is at odds with those theses. Is it therefore less tempting than we might have expected? (Indeed, has that been true of each form of nominalism? If so, should we accept Platonic Realism? That is hardly a philosophically straightforward prospect either. Understanding the world's metaphysical foundations is far from easy.)

Question 6.5 'Because everyone is different, no one can accurately judge another.' But if there are recurring, shared, properties, then not all persons are wholly different from each other. Is this a good enough basis upon which to begin understanding each other? And does the existence of those shared properties help us to assess the moral significance of others' actions? (If we share the properties of being a person and being susceptible to pain, is this a sufficient basis upon which to make some correct or warranted moral assessments? Would it be morally irrelevant that people differ widely in such respects as height or intelligence, say?)

Individualised properties

Some philosophers argue that we need not accept either Platonic Realism or a form of nominalism. They offer a compromise solution to the problem of universals. Their key concept is that of an *individualised property* (or, to mention two other terms often used, *abstract particular* or *trope*).

Their idea is that there is my personhood and there is yours, for instance – and that these are genuinely individual. You and I do not literally share a property (which would therefore be a repeatable, a universal). There is no abstract, Platonic, universal of being a person, standing apart from you and me while nonetheless applying to us. Rather, each of us has a distinct property. (And if we did not exist, our individualised properties of being a person would not do so, either.) Our two individualised properties do happen to resemble each other, though. The way in which I am a person is very similar to the way in which you are one. This is why both of us are persons. But again, we are not both persons because we share the one property. We do not have a common or shared nature as persons; we have only resembling natures as persons. You are a person because of your intrinsic nature – how you are within yourself. I am a person because of my intrinsic nature – how I am within myself. These intrinsic natures happen to resemble each other.

Yet there is something puzzling about those resemblance relations. Suppose that my being a person resembles yours, and that yours resembles Plato's, and so on. These are different particular instances of resemblance (linking different individualised properties of being particular persons). Now let's consider two possibilities.

First, suppose that no one of us – you, I, Plato, and so on – is any more a person than is any other one of us. Then does your being a person *exactly* resemble everyone else's being a person? If it does, is that because a single property is being manifested in these cases? Otherwise, given the vast complexity involved in being a particular person, it would be remarkable to have all of the world's particular, and varying, persons matching each other exactly as regards being a person. But if we decide that there is a single property being repeated, we are accepting Platonic Realism. We would have discarded the idea that all properties are particular, individualised.

Second, suppose, instead, that there is only ever an approximate – an inexact – resemblance between the many different instances of being a person – your being a person, my being one, and so on. If there are merely approximate resemblances in respect of being a person, though, are there degrees of personhood? And if so, are some of us persons to a higher degree than others? Are you more – or are you less – a person than someone else? Some will find that a disturbing thought. But can we fully eliminate it if we accept that all properties are individualised?

Question 6.6 'There but for the grace of God go I.' Many people speak like that. Yet do they really mean it? Are people who are born into wealth *essentially* wealthy? Could they have been born into poverty instead, still being the same person? If so, then even though that did not actually happen, should they have a humbling sense of the luck that has shaped their lives? What of people who, through talent and/or hard work and/or blatant luck, have become rich? If there was a possibility of their not gaining that wealth, should they retain some humility over having done so? ('But I worked hard. I deserve it.' 'Yes, and did you have no luck? Without that luck, where would you be now? Is all hard work so well rewarded?')

Essentialism

Whatever properties are, exactly, this much is clear: A given property characterises whatever has it. And sometimes properties – or so it has seemed to many philosophers over the centuries – characterise especially deeply. *Essentialism* is the thesis that some individual things have some properties essentially. Your essential properties are those that you literally could not have lacked while still being you. In this way, they help to constitute your numerical identity (a concept introduced in Chapter 1 (Questions of personal identity)): you could not lack them over time without ceasing literally to be you. We might call their combination your *essence*. Do you also have some properties inessentially – those not belonging to your essence? Your inessential properties (or, as philosophers call them, your *accidental* ones) are those that you could have lacked while still being you. Although you have them, you did not *have* to do so in order to be you.

Many of our properties, it seems, are inessential to us. Presumably, if you dye your hair a new colour, you do not cease to exist, being replaced by a new person. There would be a qualitative change in you, without there being a numerical change of person. Some cases, however, are less simple. It can be hard to know which, if any, of an individual's properties are part of his or her or its essence. Here are three important and subtle cases.

Gender   Could you have been born with a different gender from your actual one? Would that hypothetical person still have been you? Quite a few people have undergone gender transformation, to some extent or other. And generally we are content to say that numerically the one person has persisted: 'and then he was a she' (applying Lou Reed's famous lyric, from his song 'Take a Walk on the Wild Side', to this case). Yes, dramatic qualitative changes will have occurred. Still, if the persistence of other properties – which ones? – suffices for the one person to have persisted, then his or her original gender was not essential to her or him. (Would this imply, too, that no one's gender is essential to them?) On the other hand, is it possible that, in a gender transformation case, one person has literally been replaced by a second person? If it is, then the specific gender was essential after all. (The person-after-the-process could well feel that he or she is the same person as the person-before-the-process and the person-at-each-stage-during-the-process. Or the later person might feel like literally a new person. Are such feelings decisive? Or could a person be mistaken as to whether he or she was essentially a she or a he?)

Cultures   There are different reasons people might have for wishing to restrict immigration to their country. One reason could be a desire for the country's racial or cultural mix to remain unaltered. That reason may be expressed in these terms:

> We should allow no immigration from countries whose usual cultural practices are clearly different to ours. Only thus can our culture remain as it is.

This is a radically essentialist way of talking about a country's culture. It is radically essentialist because it regards *any* change to the cultural mix as 'killing' the culture – as replacing a culture with one that is qualitatively distinct *and* thereby numerically distinct.

Is there any plausibility in that way of conceiving of a country's cultural mix? It might depend upon the specific culture, and upon which possible changes are contemplated. Maybe a comparatively closed and homogeneous culture has more features that are essential to it than does a comparatively open and heterogeneous culture. For instance, suppose that you classify the democratic freedoms of expression and assembly as essential to your country's culture. (They might be required by your country's constitution or common law.) Does this commit you to some flexibility in your view of who may live in your country and how they may do so? If it does, you would have to accept that the particular mix of persons and cultures within your country at a particular time is an accidental – inessential – property of it. You would therefore be committed to rejecting the radically essentialist reasoning noted two paragraphs ago. (But this is not to say that you could never consistently object to particular cases of immigration. If the values of free expression and assembly are essential to your country, possibly any immigrants who disdain those values are a threat to that culture's literal identity.)

Love   In loving someone, what is it about them that you love? 'I love some of their properties – that smile, the calmness, and so on.' Would you therefore love anyone else who happens to have those properties? That sounds like a worryingly vulnerable love. 'No, I love the particular combination of properties which only my beloved has.' A person's properties can change over time, though, replacing one combination with another: appearances change, as do characters. Will your love be correlatively transient? Would you need to love fresh combinations of properties – time and again? (Would your love need to be born anew – time and again?) And will this increase the risk of your ceasing to love that person, whenever they have a new combination of properties which you do not love? 'No, because among those properties I love are some that are *essential* to my beloved. Other properties might depart; these ones cannot. I love the essential aspects of my beloved's character. They will never leave.' But how easy is it to know which properties are essential to the person you love? What are the unchangeable aspects of your beloved's character? How do you know that there are any? Only limited evidence for thinking that a person is essentially fair-minded, say, is available, certainly early in a relationship. So, do we tend to love people on dangerously restricted evidence? Can we therefore never know that we love someone? (Whether this rather disturbing possibility is actualised depends on what knowledge is – something we begin thinking about in Chapter 9.)

Further reading

On the problem of universals:

> D.M. Armstrong, *Nominalism and Realism*, vol. I of *Universals and Scientific Realism* (Cambridge: Cambridge University Press, 1978).
>
> D.M. Armstrong, *Universals: An Opinionated Introduction* (Boulder, CO: Westview Press, 1989).
>
> Michael J. Loux (ed.), *Universals and Particulars: Readings in Ontology* (Garden City, NY: Anchor Books, 1970).
>
> E.J. Lowe, *A Survey of Metaphysics* (Oxford: Oxford University Press, 2002), ch. 19.
>
> Bertrand Russell, *The Problems of Philosophy* (Oxford: Clarendon Press, 1959 [1912]), chs IX, X.

For Plato on Forms:

> Plato, *Phaedo* 65d–66a, 73b–79a, 96a–107b; *Republic* 478e–480a, 507a–511e, 596a–597d; *Parmenides* 130a–135b. (These are among the more prominent passages in which Plato investigates hypotheses about the nature of Forms.)

On individualised properties:

> Keith Campbell, *Abstract Particulars* (Oxford: Blackwell, 1990).

On essential properties:

> Saul A. Kripke, *Naming and Necessity* (Cambridge, MA: Harvard University Press, 1980).
>
> E.J. Lowe, *A Survey of Metaphysics*, ch. 6.
>
> Alvin Plantinga, *The Nature of Necessity* (Oxford: Clarendon Press, 1974), chs II–IV.

7

Truth

Caring about truth as such

Do you care about truth? 'Of course,' you reply. But should you feel sure of that? Might only what *you* think is true – hence, only some particular possible truths – be important to you? Maybe only those truths matter to you that are endorsed by people you like or by those with whom you share a close bond. If these are your real concerns, you do not care about truth *as such*. (You would be like those so-called sports fans whose support for a favoured team never permits them to accept that a penalty awarded against their team is deserved.)

One way to test whether you care about truth as such is to ask yourself why you want to be right in your beliefs or claims (for short: your *views*). Tell yourself, 'I want to be right in whatever I think or say.' Now reflect on why you have that desire. It is easy to confuse the idea of caring for truth – caring about being right – with any of these:

'I want to believe or feel that I am right.'
'I want other people to think that I am right.'
'I care about being the first to find the truth on a given topic.'
'I want to be right – and other people to be wrong.'
'I want to be right so that I can feel pleased with myself.'
'I care about being right so that I can be powerful.'

If what you really want is to be right for any of these reasons, then your wanting to be right is not your caring about truth as such. Again, do you respect truth as such?

It might depend on what truth is. Let's assume that it is a property, possessed by some thoughts and claims. How do we determine or know which views are true? In the next chapter, we start answering that question; this chapter asks only what sort of property truth is. This is an ancient question, almost imponderable. We may begin with some understanding of what truth is not. When you have a belief or make a claim, the truth of that view is not your thinking or feeling that it is true. Nor is its seeming to others to be true. It is not your feeling pleased at having that belief or making that claim. And it is not your having the power to force others to share your view. We know that truth is different from these various properties, if we know that to care about these is not to care about truth as such – truth in itself, truth for its own sake, truth-no-matter-which-particular-views-happen-to-be-true.

But if truth is not identical to any of these, what is it? Why is it not just others agreeing with you? Why is it not simply the opinion of some powerful person? When a belief of yours is true, which of its properties constitute its being true?

Question 7.1   If most people were to believe the earth as a whole to be flat, would that belief therefore be true? Or are honest and widespread opinions sometimes false? ('Our beliefs do not directly affect the shape of the earth.') When first you meet a new group of people, should you – would you – assume that most of their views are true? Should you react less generously if you cannot understand their language? Or must you assume that they see the world much as you do, if you are to translate what they are saying? (If they had a very different interpretation of the world, could you ever understand them?)

Correspondence

Sitting down, you think, unexcitedly but accurately, 'I am sitting down.' According to probably the oldest and most popular philosophical analysis of truth – the *correspondence* theory – your thought is true because it *corresponds to the fact* of your sitting down. There is that fact; here is your thought; your thought has a content ('what it says'); and that content is true because it is made true by that fact. Your thought is true of part – a 'piece' – of the world. Your thought accurately describes some part of the world. The fact of your sitting down is that part of the world. It is just one among many parts: the world is full of facts. Perhaps the world amounts to a jigsaw puzzle of interlocking facts and their parts (which might often include, say, individuals with properties). And the correspondence theory – the basic idea of which was espoused by Aristotle, for one – makes truth and falsity answerable to those facts.

In distinguishing facts from truths, the correspondence theory is careful where often ordinary speech is not. It is easy to talk of truths and facts indiscriminately and confusedly. (I recall reading of a politician's saying that the facts did not match up with what actually happened!) But philosophers must be more exact. The terms 'truth' and 'fact' are handy ones with which to name these two elements of what has traditionally been thought to be a fundamental metaphysical distinction:

> *Truths*: Accurate representations or depictions. (Must these be linguistic in form?)
> *Facts*: Whatever can be accurately represented or depicted by truths.

Truths are true thoughts or claims – true views. Facts are not. The correspondence theory says that when a truth is thought or spoken, a corresponding fact in the world is making that thought or claim true. In this way, truths cannot exist without facts.

But perhaps facts can exist without truths. The correspondence theory's metaphysical picture allows there to be facts which exist without being accurately represented or depicted in thought or speech. Facts make views true once we have those views; until we do, though, a particular fact might exist anyway, escaping our notice. In this sense, the correspondence theory accommodates the idea of there being *objective* truths. This is not a matter of some truths being obviously true to many people; for instance, a view might be objectively true without anyone's realising that it is. When a view is objectively true, this is because (says the correspondence theory) it corresponds – regardless of whether anyone has further evidence of its doing so – to a fact which would exist even if no one had ever thought of, or described, that fact. When forming beliefs or making claims, we hope that they are true; but our hoping that they are true rarely constitutes their being true. Philosophers tend to interpret the concept of objective truth in accordance with the correspondence theory.

Not all philosophers think of truth in that way, though. Are some views true without corresponding to facts? Here are two candidates.

Negative facts   It is true that you are not a koala. So, is there a fact of your not being a koala? Can you picture that fact – making sure that you are not picturing some merely similar or related fact, such as your not being a possum, or your being a person? If the world is just whatever *is*, how can it contain something that is *not*?

Moral facts   Most of us believe that racism is morally wrong, say. Is that belief made true by the world's containing a corresponding fact of racism's being morally wrong? Philosophers have struggled with the question of what would constitute a moral fact. For example, are there properties of being racist and of being morally wrong, with some actions having the former – and thereby the latter – property? Can we observe instances of these properties – a particular action's being immoral-because-racist? Even if we cannot observe this, can the fact of racism's being immoral exist anyway? How would it do so?

Question 7.2   Can people have culturally distinctive views that are false? 'Yet those views could matter greatly to them.' 'It's unfortunate, then, if the world is such that people have misdescribed it in important ways.' Or is it impossible – and do we know this in advance of investigating any specific cases – for that fate to befall a culturally identified group of people? Are all culturally distinctive beliefs true?

Coherence

If the correspondence theory is correct, in principle you could have a *single* true belief or make a *single* true claim – either of which might be true without your having *evidence* of its being so. Your view could *be* true – simply by corresponding to the appropriate fact. Your having another true belief or making another true claim is not needed; nor, therefore, is your having other views supporting the first one. Every so often, however, dissatisfaction with that picture leads a philosopher to endorse a *coherence* theory of truth. This says that a view is true only insofar as it belongs to a coherent system of other views – which would themselves be true for the same reason, by belonging to that same coherent system. (This will be a system of many of your own views, perhaps also of others' views.) So, if you have one true view, you have many. On the coherence theory's interpretation, no correspondence with an 'external' fact is required for truth; a mutually supportive relationship with kindred beliefs or claims suffices. Thus, the only views that are true are those that we can *support* – via *other* true views (true in the same way) – as being true.

For instance, a coherence theorist might say that a scientific theory's being true is its logically harmonising with associated theses, such as predictions – not its corresponding to some fact 'out there' (perhaps a complicated one). Is scientific truth nothing more than science's telling an extended and internally consistent story? Similarly, is moral truth just one's having a suitably large and integrated body of moral and related views? Is moral truth merely an extended and internally consistent moral story?

Here are two questions, though, about the coherence theory's scope.

Observational views   Even if some truth is coherence, perhaps some is correspondence instead. Observational views, for example, report or arise from observational interactions with the surrounding world: 'I see a cat,' 'That's a wallaby,' and so on. Is 'I see a cat' true simply by 'fitting together' with other thoughts or remarks that seem to be about cats, animals, and seeing? Shouldn't your claim 'I see a cat' also cohere with your *experience*, apparently of seeing a cat? Yet if that experience does not in turn 'cohere with the fact' of your seeing a cat, then (we might well think) your claim is not true. And isn't this another way of requiring your claim to *correspond* to a fact if it is to be true?

Competing systems   The following classic objection denies that coherence theories adequately analyse even some truth. Suppose that two people disagree, ostensibly about some aspect of reality. (For instance, one says that human beings evolved from apes; the other denies this.) And suppose that they tell equally internally coherent stories (each story having an equally good 'internal logic'). Nonetheless, because they disagree, they cannot both be right. Having internally consistent and extensive views on some topic, therefore, is not enough to make those views true. Even when views are true, this is not simply *because* they belong to an internally coherent gathering of views.

Many significant situations exemplify that objection to coherence theories. Someone who believes that there is a God might interpret his or her experiences so as never to challenge that belief. Or someone's racist beliefs could 'colour' his or her other views and experiences, with an internally coherent body of beliefs emerging, centred upon those core racist ones. The same can be true of politically painted pictures of reality. A 'conspiracy theorist', similarly, might construct a detailed and consistent theory. Or maybe someone's 'commonsense' includes his or her rejecting all unusual thoughts – such as puzzling philosophical ones! In such cases, the result might be an internally coherent system of beliefs, claims, even experiences. And if these people's views, although mutually supportive, need not be true, then being mutually supportive is also not enough to make any of *your* views true. If you have true views, this is not what makes them true.

Of course, when wishing to know which of our views are true, we seek independent indications – separate criteria – of truth. And several views' cohering with each other is indeed an indication of their being true. That is, it is some evidence of truth. But this by itself, it seems, does not *make* them true. Insofar as coherence theories are inadequate in principle, we should not confuse a view's being true with our having evidence for its being true. ('Can we ever understand the nature of evidence, though, distinguishing it clearly from truth?' In the next chapter we try to do so.)

Question 7.3   Is it possible for people everywhere to agree on a finished and complete body of views as to what reality is like – yet for everyone to be mistaken, somewhere in those views? Might such a mistake never be discovered, even over the entirety of human history? If you were guaranteed that everyone would always agree with you, would this make your views true? (What if other people are aiming for nothing more as thinkers than agreement among themselves?) Are some people better than others at accurately representing reality?

Pragmatism

Beginning late in the nineteenth century, some of America's most famous philosophers (notably, C.S. Peirce, William James, and John Dewey) began fashioning *pragmatist* conceptions of many important phenomena. Truth was one such phenomenon. There are different versions of pragmatism, built around the idea of *instrumentalism*. This tells us that beliefs and claims are tools – instruments – to be used. True beliefs and claims are those with appropriate causal consequences. They are the ones that work. They work profitably, as the tools they are intended to be. They make a discernible difference (if not immediately, then over time) to the quality of the lives of those people using them. We might say that a true view is essentially or intrinsically useful – as against accidentally or extrinsically so. That is, we might say that, necessarily and in itself, truth is a useful property for a view to have – and so it is the view's *being* useful. Pragmatism thus aims to explain why truth is something about which to *care*: We value whatever shapes our lives usefully – which is precisely what truth does (say pragmatists). Truth *is* what truth *does*.

Yet few philosophers, it seems, now think that pragmatism portrays truth's core. Perhaps it just describes some further properties of some true views. Is being-useful what makes a belief or claim true? Maybe instead it is merely why we *care* about whether our views are true. Even when it is useful for people to believe that they are especially intelligent, for example, this does not make it true that they are very intelligent – no matter how much they wish themselves to be. Moreover, if we assume that a view's being true is its being useful, are we unable to distinguish useful truths from useless ones? This is a distinction we seem to find useful, though.

In any case, what is it for a view to be useful? Because there is no single pragmatist answer to that question, we must think about it in a general way. Here are some interrelated questions and suggestions.

Substantive usefulness   All of your beliefs and claims – true or not – contribute somehow to your living as a person. All of them – true or not – affect what experiences you have. Are all of them therefore useful to your life? Lives can proceed in better or worse ways; and if a view is to be true by being useful, presumably it needs to be substantively useful. It needs to contribute well, making a real difference to the quality of your life. But what makes a view substantively useful?

Correspondence   One suggestion is that a view can make a real difference to your life by accurately reflecting the world in which you live, such as by allowing you to make accurate predictions. (For then you do not continually 'bump into' the world.) However, this suggestion collapses the pragmatist theory back into a correspondence theory.

Coherence   Another suggestion is that a view is useful insofar as it fits well with your other views, including your other experiences. (For example, you might defend religious beliefs as being true in a pragmatist way, by saying that, regardless of whether they correspond to independent facts, they are useful to people's lives. They cause feelings of supposedly spiritual pleasure or satisfaction. They reinforce beliefs about the world's nature and point. Or you might defend scientific beliefs as being pragmatically true, claiming that they explain why we have the experiences we do. They 'fit together' with our experiences.) This suggestion, though, collapses the pragmatist theory back into a coherence theory.

Non-truth   A view could also be useful by being almost true, or by not being noticeably false, or by being enjoyable to have, and so on. Yet such properties are rarely, if ever, enough to make the view true.

Ultimately, therefore, pragmatist theories of truth have the same failing as we found (at the end of the previous section) afflicting coherence theories. They tell us more about some indications or criteria of truth than about its inherent nature. Whether a view is useful is *evidence* of its being true. This does not equal the view's being true.

Question 7.4   'I respect your right to say that you're not guilty.' In your own mind, you're not guilty.' Is this a tolerant and understanding way to talk to someone? Or is it condescending and patronising? Imagine the person replying thus: 'It isn't just in my own mind that I'm innocent. I really didn't do the damn deed.' Is this person revealing that he or she believes there to be some objective truths? In which circumstances do people apparently manifest a commitment to there being such truths?

Disagreement

I have been assuming that truth exists, with us wanting to understand its metaphysical nature. But is it possible that there is no truth? Or might it be that when we use the word 'true' we refer to some weaker kind of truth? The usual suggestion to this effect is that your views are true for you, mine are true for me, and similarly for everyone else's. There would be no truth 'out there' – because there would be no facts 'out there'. There would be only subjective truth (or relative truth, or perspectival or partial truth). Might there not be even that? Should we replace the idea of truth with something else?

These dramatic thoughts deny, in effect, that there is any objective truth (the kind characterised by the correspondence theory). The most common reason people have, it seems, for making that denial is the existence of *disagreements* over what is true. (These could be caused by many factors, including differences of cultural background, race, class, gender, perceptual or intellectual capacities or 'inputs', emotional preferences, and so on.) Here are six unsettling inferences people might draw from the existence of disagreements – along with explanations of why, quite rightly, few philosophers are impressed by those inferences.

'Because people disagree, there is no truth at all.' But disagreement as to what is true does not entail that nothing is true. It entails that not all of the people involved are correct. It does not entail that none of them is, let alone that no one anywhere is.

'Because people disagree, who is ever to say who is right?' This is claiming that no one could know whose view is correct. Yet even if, in a given situation, we cannot know whose view is correct, this does not entail no one's *being* correct. (Maybe it is not true, anyway, that no one ever knows. It depends on what knowledge is – our topic in Chapter 9.)

'Because it is disrespectful to assume that those with whom one disagrees are mistaken, no one is right and no one is wrong.' It is disrespectful to *assume* that others are mistaken. Even so, they still might be mistaken. And it is not always disrespectful to disagree with other people. You could engage respectfully with another's claims, remaining genuinely open to the possibility of being mistaken yourself – before concluding, in good faith, that the other person is mistaken. In any event, disrespect is beside the point; it is possible to be rude yet correct. (I am not advocating rudeness, of course. I am noting only that being false is not always one of its failings.)

'Because – especially in a politically or ethnically pluralist society – we should tolerate alternative viewpoints, including those with which we disagree, no one is right and no one is wrong.' But even when a society accords differing views an equal political right to be heard, this does not guarantee that all of those views are correct. Many of them might be badly mistaken. (Just listen to 'talkback radio' – or some academics – for a while.) A civil society allows citizens opportunities to develop opinions and to speak their minds, even on politically sensitive topics. However, having both a chance to think and a right to speak will not ensure one's gaining views that are true. A person can feel correct without being correct; a political right to think and speak freely can coexist with this possibility. It could be thought of as the political right to think and speak absolute truths *or* – for whatever reason (including insufficient talent or thought) – absolute falsehoods. (It would be each person's political right to be uninformed and wrong!) If we deny that anyone is ever really mistaken, we deny – maybe unwittingly – that anyone is ever really right. No deeply civil society would do that. Deep tolerance includes accepting that others' views could be true, really true – and that one's own views could be false, really false. To deny that there is real truth ('because everyone is right in his or her own way') is impliedly to deny that there is real falsity, including – ever – one's own falsity. This is not deeply tolerant of alternative viewpoints.

'Because people disagree, there are different realities. (It's all relative.)' However, this claim is either incoherent or trivial. It is incoherent if it is saying that there are literally different realities; for reality is whatever exists. And the claim is trivial if it means just that there are competing opinions on what reality is like. Of course there are; this banal point merely returns us to the first of our six inferences.

'Because people disagree, truth must be "in between" the differing viewpoints.' Unfortunately, this inference is a popular response to deep or complex disagreements. There is a temptation to think that because no one will ever disentangle the warring opinions, truth must be 'in the middle'. ('The truth no doubt contains elements from all of those positions.') But that is poor reasoning. If it is all 'too hard to work out', there is no more entitlement to locate the truth 'in between' than 'at one end'. Truth as such *could* be wholly with one side of a debate.

We should concede that disagreements do indeed constitute some evidence of the contested views not being true. But they are not always strong evidence of that; it depends upon each particular case's details. So they rarely, if ever, *prove* that truth is absent. Correspondence theorists would say that this is because disagreements rarely, if ever, *constitute* truth's being absent: one view might correspond to a fact by reporting it accurately – while the other view unwittingly does not.

Question 7.5   Often people who seek political changes in the name of political progress reject the idea of objective truth. ('Truth only aids those in power. It's a reactionary concept. We must discard the whole idea of truth.') Yet if all claims to truth merely mouth political preferences, can there be real political progress? Does such progress require there to be genuine facts upon which to improve and genuine facts as to what would constitute an improved society – for example, facts as to what hardships, particularly undeserved ones, have occurred in the past, and facts as to which outcomes, hopefully good ones, are possible? (Otherwise, there would be no facts of women, or of any religious or racial groups, ever having been oppressed, say.) So, are calls for progress that jettison the idea of objective truth undermining their own credibility? Must they regard themselves as merely ideological preferences – as not objectively true? If so, are they pure rhetoric too – perhaps emotionally moving, and little else? Does 'shallow' politics ignore real truth? Does 'substantive' politics at least seek it?

Claiming truth

Some of the mistakes mentioned in the previous section rest upon a simple confusion, which we avoid by distinguishing between *claiming* to be correct and a claim's *being* correct. There is *claiming a truth*, and there is *a claim's being true*. Someone's claiming a truth is some slight evidence of their claim's being true; but rarely does it *make* their claim true. Keeping this distinction in mind should avert various fundamental misconceptions.

Suppose that I say you have a free will – and that I am right. Nevertheless, aspects of a conversational situation could make me withdraw my claim – even though, had I not withdrawn it, my claim would have been true. Disagreements provoke everyday instances of that sort of situation. If people are talking philosophically about whether you have a free will, and if they disagree, they could become so unconfident about the issue as to be unwilling to say, one way or the other, whether you have a free will. However, that does not change the reality of whether you *have* a free will. If you had one, you continue doing so.

Now imagine, instead, my ignoring the objections voiced by others in that discussion: in spite of their disagreeing with me, I maintain my claim that you have a free will. And my claim could be true, even when others reject it. I will probably find it hard to convince those other people of the truth of my claim about you. Again, though, this would not entail its being false. Maybe my continuing to describe you as I do, being unpersuaded by the objections to my view, would mark my being somewhat dogmatic on this occasion, as I deeply and unremittingly believe that you have a free will. But what of it? Dogmatism can lead to truth. Most likely, it does so less often than open-mindedness does; nonetheless, it can do so. Personal niceties and social graces (or, less admirably, a mere desire to 'fit in') could induce someone to withdraw his or her claims once others disagree with them. Yet unless all truth is as social as that, your deferring so accommodatingly to others might deprive you of a true claim about the world.

Question 7.6   As a speaker, is your main aim to be correct? Or do you only seek to be friendly to others? If you had to choose between those two goals, which would you pursue? Is there a difference between treating other people respectfully and being friendly to them? Does respect always involve evaluating – without automatically accepting – the truth of what they say? Does friendliness involve that only sometimes?

Social constructivism

Might it be, then, that all truth *is* social? This is a currently popular idea in such university departments as those of sociology, anthropology, literature, cultural studies, communication, gender studies, and race studies, among others. Some philosophers also embrace it. Usually, it is called *social constructivism* about truth. It is a kind of *relativism*. (We meet that way of thinking again in Chapter 8 (Epistemic relativism). Many people deem such relativist views to be a vital part of *postmodernism*.) Social constructivism is a relativist view because it regards any view's being true as depending just upon whether different social or cultural groupings think that it is true – so that even if a view is deemed true by one group and not by another, neither group is thereby mistaken. (Social constructivism is an adaptation of label nominalism, too, a view outlined in Chapter 6 (Label nominalism). For it makes truth a matter only of whether a particular social or cultural grouping accepts a given belief or claim – a matter of how people attempt to *label* the world.)

Here is perhaps the strongest way in which social constructivism about truth might be developed:

> Truths are expressed linguistically. Yet languages are *social constructs*: people created them. Accordingly, languages embody cultural realities, reflecting parochialisms and partialities. So, we never express truths in a neutral way. We report on the world only through our socially constructed – and correlatively restricted – ways of speaking and thinking. We cannot 'escape' those social influences. Whatever truths we express are thus socially imbued. And this matters, because whatever is socially constructed need not have been. There is an arbitrariness to any particular social construction: we could have developed different languages and accepted different views expressed in those languages. There is therefore an arbitrariness to truth. Because we create truths, we can control and change them. What is true today need not be true tomorrow, as we adopt new ways of talking and thinking.

In order to assess that reasoning's quality, let's grant its starting-point. We may agree that any truth expressed linguistically is formulated in some socially created and transmitted language. This commits us to conceding that the truth expressed by 'You are a person' is indeed a social construct – in a narrow sense. For we should concede that the *claim*, and maybe the *thought*, that you are a person is formulated, and hence exists, via social tools – namely, words. If so, then truths – in the sense of true *views*, expressed by actual people – exist because, in part, of social facts. However, few philosophers would then infer that what *makes* someone's view true (given how it is expressed) is always partly or wholly social. Even if the claim that you are a person is socially constructed, whatever makes that claim true need not be. The fact of your having various properties might be what makes you a person. If so, this also makes true the view (once someone has it) that you are a person.

But even if no one ever has that view, the fact remains that you are a person anyway. (To deny this is to return to the conventionalism discussed in Chapter 1 (Conventionalism). If that seemed false, so should social constructivism.) As we might put the point (applying the section, Claiming truth): We should not confuse what makes a stated truth true with what is needed for stating that truth. Social constructivists seem to be guilty of some such confusion.

They are careless, similarly, about distinguishing facts from truths. It is natural to distinguish (as the correspondence theory does) between a *fact* of your being a person, and a *truth* being formulated or claimed by the English sentence 'You are a person', for instance. But many social constructivists claim, more or less openly, that all *reality* is socially constructed. There are no facts other than social ones (we are told). Why would that be so? Is it because we cannot describe a fact other than linguistically? Is it because we reflect some social background when choosing what to describe? Is it because our evidence as to what is true is socially produced – and restricted? None of these considerations proves that there are no non-social facts, though. Those facts (yes, facts) just remind us that – for many reasons, including social ones – no particular person or society or culture is guaranteed to know, or to describe accurately, all of the world's facts. There is much that can affect which, if any, of the world's facts we know.

Of course, we did not need social constructivists to remind us of this. We already knew it. The correspondence theory, most notably, allows there to be facts that would have existed even if language or thought had not done so: these are facts we might never have described or known, just as presumably there are facts we will never describe or know. We did not make the world. Not even with language and thought have we done so. Words and thoughts are not *that* powerful. If future generations of people choose to deny that the Nazi Holocaust occurred, will they be socially constructing the world anew? Not at all: perhaps some future people will not have in mind the truth of the horrors that occurred; once the Holocaust has happened, though, future words – future social constructing – cannot make it 'unhappen'. Those facts of the Holocaust remain, no matter whether future social arrangements prevent future people from knowing what happened. History-as-those-facts remains whatever it was in itself, even when history-as-true-views-recording-those-facts has become disputed – or has even disappeared.

Question 7.7 Is a view not racist or sexist, for example, if it is true? Is being mistaken – genuinely, objectively mistaken – essential to a view's being racist or sexist? Maybe there are truths, at least partly about race or gender, that cannot be uttered in many contexts without being rude or causing distress to some people. But would that be enough to make those truths racist or sexist? (There is no sexism or racism simply in making a claim about males or females in general, or about members in general of some racially characterised group. A view can have a racial subject, for instance, without being racist, and there can be true views with a racial subject.)

Social facts

Social constructivists mistakenly think that reality always reflects how we think about it; or so the previous section argued. Nevertheless, does *some* reality possess that characteristic? Are some facts partly social (even if not all facts have that feature)? Are there facts that exist only because people regard them as doing so (thereby giving them a social function)?

For instance, is a shop a shop partly because people think that it is? It does play a designated social role: it is not merely a physical construction. Still (and here we remind ourselves of why social constructivism is false), a shop is a shop only *partly* because of how people regard it. Given how society functions at present, we could not treat just anything as a shop. A shop must have some physical characteristics which are whatever they are in themselves, purely physically – regardless of how people think about and describe them. (This is true even of a cybershop, trading wholly over the internet.) In other words, a shop's being a shop seems to be a fact composed of two further facts – one about purely physical reality, existing independently of any social gaze being directed at it, and another that is social, as that physical reality comes to fulfil a social need because some people view it as doing so.

Suppose, then, that some reality is social, in part because of how we describe it. Does this undermine the thesis that there is objective reality? If a shop is a shop in part because we think it is, we could make it cease to be a shop – simply by our no longer viewing it as being one. Is its being a shop therefore not so real?

Certainly it is fashionable (as the section, Social constructivism, indicated) for many people to deride the ideas of objective truth and reality, as those ideas are described by the correspondence theory. But consider the following two points.

Reality   A social fact is as it is because of how we describe some reality that is not social. In creating a social fact of something's being a shop, we describe something purely physical – hence, something which is not merely a social fact – so as to make it a shop. The shop is therefore partly non-socially constituted, even if it is also partly socially constituted.

Knowledge In general, if you were not to recognise a specific shop as being a shop, wouldn't you be as mistaken as if you were to fail to recognise a particular dog as being a dog? You can know that the shop in front of you is a shop, every bit as much as you can know that the dog in front of you is a dog. Isn't this so, even if the shop's being a shop is in part a socially constructed fact, and even if the dog's being a dog is not? Even what is, in part, socially constructed can help to make views non-arbitrarily true. And it seems that at least some, maybe many, such truths can be known to be true. ('But that depends upon what knowledge is.' Yes, it does; Chapter 9 will try to ascertain what knowledge is.)

Further reading

On truth in general:
Michael Devitt, *Realism and Truth*, 2nd edn (Oxford: Blackwell, 1991).
A.C. Ewing, *The Fundamental Questions of Philosophy* (London: Routledge & Kegan Paul, 1951), ch. 3.
Alvin I. Goldman, *Knowledge in a Social World* (Oxford: Clarendon Press, 1999), ch. 2.
Robert Kirk, *Relativism and Reality: A Contemporary Introduction* (London: Routledge, 1999).
Richard L. Kirkham, *Theories of Truth: A Critical Introduction* (Cambridge, MA: The MIT Press, 1992).
George Pitcher (ed.), *Truth* (Englewood Cliffs, NJ: Prentice-Hall, 1964).

On the correspondence theory of truth:
D.J. O'Connor, *The Correspondence Theory of Truth* (London: Hutchinson, 1975).

On the coherence theory of truth:
Ralph C.S. Walker, *The Coherence Theory of Truth: Realism, Anti-Realism, Idealism* (London: Routledge, 1989).

On pragmatist theories of truth:
Hilary Putnam, *Pragmatism: An Open Question* (Oxford: Blackwell, 1995), ch. 1.

On social constructivism:
Alvin I. Goldman, *Knowledge in a Social World*, ch. 1.
Ian Hacking, *The Social Construction of What?* (Cambridge, MA: Harvard University Press, 1999).
Alan Sokal and Jean Bricmont, *Intellectual Impostures: Postmodern Philosophers' Abuse of Science* (London: Profile Books, 1998 [1997]).

On social facts:
John R. Searle, *The Construction of Social Reality* (London: Penguin, 1995).

8

Well Supported Views

Objective support

If we are to decide, as fairly and carefully as we can, which views are true, must we seek good evidence supporting some views rather than others? How well can you do that? Not all views are well supported. Not everyone has equally well supported views. In general, what are the marks of a view's being well supported?

Compare these two situations:

Myron is pleased with himself today – as he always is. Taking it for granted that his eyes are working well, he believes that he sees a cat on the other side of the road. It never occurs to him that this belief could be false. And is it? I am not saying. What I will say is that Myron's eyes are not working well today. In fact, they often fail to do so. Myron is a slow-witted person with a poor sensory grasp of the world. Yet he never realises this sobering truth about himself. (Although his eyes have always been poor, no one has ever corrected Myron's belief that he has fine eyesight.)

Beth is nervous and unconfident today – as she always is. Is that a cat over there, on the other side of the road? 'Yes,' thinks Beth – yet she remains uncertain. She believes – hesitantly. And is there a cat over there? I am not saying. What I will say is that Beth's senses are highly attuned to her surroundings – as they usually are. Although they are not infallible, they are good. Beth is an intelligent person with good observational abilities. But she never realises this uplifting truth about herself. (Her intelligence and humility lead routinely to her thinking of reasons why her views could be mistaken.)

It is reasonable to ask whether one of Myron and Beth has better support for the truth of the belief that there is a cat on the other side of the road (the 'cat-belief'). How would we answer that question more precisely, though? What criterion – or which criteria – should we use? Which aspects of these two situations are relevant to our question?

For a start, is a person's confidence a good indicator of how well supported his or her belief is? Myron is more confident in the truth of his cat-belief than Beth is in the truth of hers. Myron is satisfied that his eyes are to be trusted; Beth is perennially cautious about relying on hers. Nonetheless, Myron's cat-belief is less well supported than he thinks it is; maybe it is only poorly supported. And Beth's cat-belief is better supported than she thinks it is; is it actually quite well supported? A person's confidence, or lack of it, in a belief can be misplaced. Being confident that one's belief is well supported, for example, might reflect one's arrogance or lack of self-awareness, or an inability to admit failure, and so on. In order to have good rational support for a view, then, it is not enough to think that one has it: Myron might well lack it, although he takes himself to have it. Nor is it necessary to think that one has it: Beth might well have it, although she takes herself not to do so.

And what of *other* people's opinions on one's support for a view? Suppose that others in the community agree with Myron and Beth in their respective self-assessments. Everyone regards Myron as a fine reporter of his environment and Beth as a poor one. (Maybe sexism explains this reaction in some cases. There could be people with eyes no better than Myron's. Possibly, some just want to believe what others believe.) Does this affect how well supported Myron's and Beth's cat-beliefs are? Or is Myron's belief poorly supported, in spite of no one around him realising it? Is Beth's belief well supported, even though no one around her is aware of this?

The question is whether Beth's support for her cat-belief is *objectively* better than Myron's is for his cat-belief. That is, is Beth's support actually better than Myron's, regardless of whether anyone thinks so? Neither has perfect support; is Beth's still better than Myron's? Most epistemologists say that it can be objectively true whether or not a given person has good support for a particular belief or claim (for its being true). That is, good support could be present even if no one suspects that it is; it can be absent even if no one believes that it is. A view's being well, or its being poorly, supported is not simply a matter of opinion. Your feeling confident that some particular view of yours is well supported – by excellent evidence, say – could be wholly mistaken. It would be pleasing if our estimations of the rational strength of our views, and of other people's views, were always correct. Alas, they are not.

Myron and Beth are typical people, in that neither is fully admirable as a thinker. Myron is too confident; Beth is not confident enough. It seems that each regularly fails to realise how well, or how poorly, supported his or her beliefs are. And something is amiss whenever a belief is held, or a claim is made, more – or, indeed, less – confidently than the objective support for its being true warrants. What is amiss is a subtle disharmony. Whenever you have good support, ideally you believe or claim confidently; whenever your support is poorer, ideally you believe or claim less confidently. Of course, this is more easily advocated than achieved. It is worth advocating, though – because it is worth achieving. You should strive to improve on both Myron and Beth.

Question 8.1   People differ widely in many skills, such as artistic or athletic ones. Often these skills seem not to be wholly under a person's command: Up to a point, you either have them – or you do not, in which case you will never have them. Could the ability to support one's views well be like that? For example, are some people inherently better at finding good evidence supporting their views? Or is no one any better at that – inherently, at any rate – than anyone else? Can people improve at this during their lives? Would it occur naturally? Would it transpire only with effort and concentration – and appropriate education?

Fallibilism

In attempting to understand what it is for a view to be well supported, philosophers employ various terms to refer to that feature of a view. The term most commonly used is 'justified'. Still, that has tended to become a disputed technical term; competing terms have been suggested and analysed. So, I am using the more everyday phrase 'well supported' generically, referring to the many possible ways for a view to be well supported as being true. (A view could also be supported in ways – such as moral or practical ones – not bearing on whether it is true. They are not this chapter's subject.)

There are also many *extents* to which a view can be well supported. That is, support for a view can be better or worse. There are grades or degrees of possible support. There can even be better or worse *good* support for a view. I think that I have good support for my belief that I am Australian. I think that I have even better support for my belief that I am a person.

Accordingly, here is a fundamental distinction:

Although the concept of good support is *objective*, it is not *absolute*. Objectivity and absoluteness are different properties.

A view can rest upon support which is objectively good (because its quality is not ultimately a matter of opinion), even while that support might have been better or might have been worse. Imagine two people living in England 300 years ago, one of whom had seen ninety swans, the other of whom had observed ninety-one swans – all of those swans having been white. Each person had evidence providing what was, objectively, fairly good support for the truth of the belief that all swans are white. Nevertheless, one of them had slightly better support than the other one had for that belief's being true.

Of course, that belief was false, not true: Australia's indigenous swans are black. And how on earth (you might wonder) could there be objectively good support for a false belief or claim? It is because even good support need not *prove* that the belief or claim in question is true. Only conclusive – perfect – support does that. And support can be good without being perfect. Good support usually leaves open a possibility of that which it supports as being true nonetheless being false; this is why the support is good, not conclusive. And sometimes that possibility is actualised, with the well supported view in question actually being false. Should we therefore lift our hands skywards, in despair at the possibility that even our well supported views are false? Should we relinquish the idea of there ever being objectively good support for a view's being true?

Few philosophers encourage that radical route. (In Chapter 12 we will seriously consider it – before also rejecting it.) Most urge calm and moderation upon us. Do not think that support has to be conclusive (they say); that would be unrealistic, pointless. Accept a *fallibilism* instead. That is, accept the possibility of having *merely good* support for a view as being true. There is no disgrace in that. Merely good is good; it is just not even better still. It falls short of being conclusive support – the only kind providing objective certainty, leaving no possibility of the view it supports being false. But you might never have had such strong support for a view anyway, irrespective of whether you have sometimes *felt* certain of a view's truth. You have probably only ever had – even at best – good-but-fallibilist support for a view. Should that be worrying? Or should we think of it as opening up the following challenging opportunity?

> Whenever support is fallibilist, there is a possibility of improving it.

How might that occur? In the next three sections, I describe a few of the many ways in which there can be objectively good – and then even better – fallibilist support for a view as being true.

Question 8.2   Can you bring to mind many poorly supported beliefs you have? (Or do you have no poorly supported beliefs?) If they are so badly supported, why did you have them in the first place? And why have you never got rid of them? Has it been irrational of you to hold them? How irrational are you?

Reliabilism

Here are the gripping words from a realistic (albeit fictitious) celebrity endorsement:

> G'day. Paul Smithly here. You've all seen me swimming fast, winning for Australia. (Mate, I love this country!) Well, that's not all I've ever won. I've just bought myself an X-car – and now I'm winning with it. So can you! Take it from me; it's the best. Get into it! You'll love it.

Paul Smithly is a non-existent person – although he is depressingly similar to many other celebrities, judging by this gem of a possible advertisement. What can Smithly teach us about cars? Nothing. He is paid to endorse cars of brand X. He is no more knowledgeable about cars than are most people. But gosh, he could swim well; we must not forget that! So, wouldn't it be rational, after seeing this advertisement, to believe that X-cars are especially good? Of course not; and we all know this when we think sensibly about it. Nonetheless, having seen or heard such advertisements, many people do, it seems, proceed to form the beliefs advertisers want them to form.

I do not know whether people as a group can avoid being so influenced by advertisements. It is hardly a way of gaining well supported beliefs as to a commercial product's quality. Smithly is no authority on cars. His endorsement of X-cars owes more to money than to rigorous, impartial, testing. If your seeing Smithly grinning, with his hair just right, perhaps displaying his swimming medals, and mouthing these inanities, leads to your forming the belief that X-cars are good, you are gaining this belief in a way that falls far short of making it well supported. Hopefully, we agree on this. But now the philosophy – specifically, the epistemology – begins. For we need to understand *why* a 'Smithly-generated' belief about X-cars is not well supported.

One possible explanation – a popular one – is called *reliabilism*. A reliabilist would no doubt say that your Smithly-generated belief is formed too unreliably to be well supported. According to reliabilism, what makes a belief well supported is the belief's being reliably formed or held. This is its having been formed, or its now being held, in a way that is likely to yield *true* beliefs. Examples abound of this sort of reliability or unreliability. Beth's reliable eyesight makes her likely to gain true beliefs about her surroundings; Myron's unreliable eyesight makes him unlikely to do so. And does reliabilism help to explain why we should value good evidence highly? Is basing a view on good, rather than bad, evidence more likely to lead to views that are true? Is reliance on bad, rather than good, evidence more likely to lead to false views?

Are these likelihoods part of what *makes* some evidence good and some not so good?

At any rate, forming a belief about a product's quality on the basis of celebrity endorsements is rather unreliable – unlikely to generate mainly true beliefs about the quality of the products being endorsed. The point is not that celebrities are always mistaken; it is that they are not particularly likely to be right. This is so, even if (as is not required) they sincerely believe in the truth of what they are saying. In general, nothing in a product's being endorsed by a celebrity as being good makes it likely to *be* good. If your next-door neighbour who happens to be obsessed by cars were to endorse X-cars (paying the TV station for the privilege!), he or she would probably not cause many people to buy X-cars. Yet believing such a person might give you a better supported view as to the quality of X-cars than you would obtain by listening to Paul Smithly – our 'You name it, I'll sell it; See my agent!' celebrity, hungry for the money. Has Smithly become an expert? No. Has he fully and disinterestedly tested X-cars against other brands? Probably not. Would he endorse a rival firm's car if they were to pay him more money? Most likely. Is his word therefore to be trusted in this setting? No. Is he lying? Not exactly. Is one nevertheless acting regrettably – epistemologically speaking – if listening to Smithly is typical of how one forms views about the world and about how to live? Yes. (And how much control do you have over yourself in this respect? If you were to acknowledge that you are thinking unreliably, how simply could you correct this flaw? Chapter 12 (Being freely rational) will develop that question more forcefully.)

Question 8.3   People can mimic those features often conventionally thought to be good indicators of a person's being a trustworthy and reliable informant. (Don't many politicians and actors do this professionally? So do some teachers and businesspeople.) A serious or concerned or thoughtful expression, a winning smile, a controlled or authoritative voice, a steady gaze, stylish or fashionable or respectable clothes: are these reliable indicators of someone who should readily be believed?

Popper and testability

Many of our views begin their lives in our minds or mouths by lacking good support. We absorb views in a multitude of ways, some of them quite unreliable. We hear rumours; we have prejudices; we listen to casual talk; perhaps we experience sudden inexplicable 'flashes of inspiration'. Even normally dependable sources of views are sometimes less reliable. On a given day, your eyesight is less precise; or your attention is somewhat distracted; or your teacher is not so well-versed on that day's topic. When a view has been formed unreliably, is it condemned to remain poorly supported? Should you jettison it?

Not necessarily; sometimes an initially unsupported view can become well supported. To understand how this can occur, we might need to look beyond reliabilism. It tells us how a view is well supported by arising in some reliable way. Yet this tells us little about how a view lacking that pedigree could subsequently gain good support. 'That is easy,' you might reply, 'I would look for evidence in favour of the view. Once I find enough, the view should stay, now being well supported.' How might you approach that task?

One of the twentieth century's most influential philosophical ideas could be helpful here. The idea comes from Karl Popper (1902–94), a famous Austrian-then-British philosopher of science. He asked what distinguishes scientific views from non-scientific ones. His answer was elegant: Scientific views are testable, falsifiable. This does not mean their being false. It means just that they can be tested experimentally and observationally – via tests meant to find the theories to be false. 'False? Why false? Aren't we looking for *support* for the theories – for their being true?' Indeed we are – but indirectly. Popper's idea was that this is best done by looking directly to *reject* the theories. A theory that does not allow this is not scientific: Popper argued, for instance, that psycho-analysis and Marxism failed to be scientific, because each allows only for 'confirming instances' – direct support. Neither ever really accepts that it could be found to be false. ('You think that falsifies my theory? No, here's how I explain that case away ... yes, like every other case! Isn't that remarkable?') Anyone merely wanting confirmation of a theory – *without* genuinely looking for ways in which it could be false – will never find real support for the theory. (Think here of those university essays in which you are expected simply to find some 'authorities' whose views agree with what you want to say.) We must do better than that. And the best we can do, it seemed to Popper, is to test a theory by try-ing to find that it is false – and then, if it has so far survived this genuine testing, to accept that the theory has done the most that we could have asked of it up to now. This is not enough to make the theory true (on a correspondence theory of truth, which is what Popper accepted). But it does make the theory more or less well corroborated (to use Popper's term) *so far*. It is still 'alive'. This speaks – somehow – in support of its being true.

That is Popper's *testability* or *falsifiability* criterion of what it is to be scientific – a criterion whose basic idea is taken for granted by many scientists these days. It is fallibilist – always open to the possibility of a given scientific theory being false, no matter how much support the theory has received thus far. Can we extend the criterion, helping us to understand the nature of good fallibilist support in general? Could it help us to understand how a view that has entered your mind quite unreliably can subsequently gain support? The idea would be that you might gain some objective support for the view by actually trying to falsify it, searching for a definitive reason to reject it as objectively false. (This is like an athlete's improving by seeking, acknowledging, and trying to eliminate, mistakes in his or her technique – rather than by being content merely to reinforce what was already correct in it.) In this way, you test the view, allowing it to stay in your mind only while it is passing some genuinely critical scrutiny. You treat the view as intended to be objectively true – and so as failing, as a view, if it is not objectively true. Your not finding it to be false does not make it true. But it does gain some kind of real (not merely apparent) support – from its so far surviving your testing. When views arise from hunches, guesses, biases, inattention, and so on, this might be the best support you can find for them.

Question 8.4   Is a view not racist or sexist, for example, if it is well supported? Is being inadequately supported – objectively poorly supported – essential to a view's being racist or sexist? Maybe there are views, at least partly about race or gender, that cannot be investigated in many contexts – as one seeks to ascertain whether good support can be found for the view in question – without being rude or without causing distress to some people. But would that be enough to make those views racist or sexist? (There is no sexism or racism simply in making a claim about males or females in general, or about members in general of some racially characterised group. A view can have a racial subject, for instance, without being racist, and there can be well supported views with a racial subject.)

Intellectual virtue

According to some philosophers, when you have a well supported view, this is because you are thinking or speaking as you *should*, given the circumstances. What does this 'should' mean? Can we interpret it analogously to how we interpret the same term when talking about *morality* – when we say that to act morally is to do what you should do, given the circumstances? In short, perhaps intellectual virtues are analogous to moral virtues. Maybe having good support for a view is at least sometimes a matter of thinking or speaking intellectually virtuously. Let's make the issue deeper still: Must you be somewhat morally good if you are to have well supported views? Possibly, some intellectual virtues actually *are* moral virtues. Do some intellectual failings indicate moral failings? Here is an example to ponder.

Recently (in 2002), an Australian politician relied on parliamentary privilege (which protects politicians from being sued for damages arising from any personal claims they make in Parliament about other people) to make accusations – of using government cars for homosexual liaisons with underage prostitutes – against a widely respected, and openly homosexual, High Court judge. The documentation used by the politician as evidence was soon found to be forged (not by him, presumably). No one continued supporting his case. Nonetheless, his defenders (all in his own government party) spoke on his behalf, along these lines:

> He meant well. We know he didn't really check on the facts. But he spoke sincerely; he really cares about the issue of paedophilia. He's a good man.

To which I reply: No, he is not a good man. If he was so good, he would have checked the reliability of his evidence before publicly damning someone. This would not have been hard to do. (Once he made the evidence public, only a day or so was needed before the evidence was seen – through parliamentary means – to be false.) The sorry fact is that this politician was intellectually reckless in his claims about the judge. He did not care sufficiently about truth as such. Clearly, his view about the judge was formed unreliably. It arose, in part, because the politician believed what he wanted to believe – never seriously testing his evidence, seeking to falsify it. This was not how someone seeking truth – objective truth – should think and speak. It was far from intellectually virtuous. There is an intellectual virtue not only in caring about truth, but in carefully testing one's evidence. That virtue was conspicuously absent from this case.

A related moral virtue was absent, too. There is a lack of moral virtue in criticising other people, in either speech or thought, without exercising the intellectual virtue of real respect for truth and evidence. Caring about other people involves caring about truth and associated intellectual virtues. It implies caring about being accurate and well supported in what one thinks and says about others. Caring about preventing paedophilia (as the politician claimed to do) is obviously admirable; in the circumstances, though, this did not make his views intellectually admirable. Nor, therefore, did it make his action of giving voice to them morally admirable. Moral virtues, it seems to many philosophers, are not just a matter of having good intentions (such as that of thwarting paedophilia). It is also important to have a reliable habit of acting well in pursuit of that intention. (Aristotle, for one, viewed moral virtues in this way.) A morally virtuous person is, in part, one with a habit of effectively doing good deeds – not just one who wants, no matter how strongly, to be like that.

Question 8.5   If a person ceases to care about finding truth as such, does this make it more likely that he or she will cease being good at finding it? Will the person's views become more likely to be poorly supported? Can people become less intelligent, observant, insightful, imaginative – and therefore less usefully accurate – throughout life? ('Use it – or lose it.') Can this occur without one's being aware of its happening? What can one do to lower its likelihood?

Agreement

We saw (in Chapter 7 (Disagreement)) that even when people disagree as to what is true, real truth – objective truth – might still exist. Nevertheless, even if disagreeing with others need not deprive you of truth, does it affect how well *supported* your beliefs and claims are? If others disagree with you, and if you cannot be certain that they are mistaken, perhaps your views are not as well supported as you might have thought. Should you therefore, as someone seeking well supported views, *agree* with others? Does believing and saying what most other people believe and say make your views well supported?

It depends. There is little, if any, inherent support for a view in its being agreed with by other people. If they themselves are poor at gaining true beliefs or making true claims, then – even if they sincerely seek truth – one's agreeing with them is not a reliable way to reach truth oneself. If the other people do not rigorously examine and test their own views, your sharing those views hardly makes them well supported. A view might be politically or culturally well supported, for example, in virtue of many people agreeing with it. But this is no guarantee of its being intellectually well supported. There is not always a rational 'safety in numbers'. People might even be unintentionally misleading each other, reinforcing shared yet mistaken views on some topic. Even when trying to correct each other, they could fail.

Question 8.6   Should an accusation of racism or sexism be based on better evidence than an accusation of impoliteness requires, for instance? How much more, if any, objectively good support is needed for a claim that a person is racist or sexist than is called for when describing a specific action or view as racist or sexist? What kinds of evidence are necessary in such cases? Are there infallible perspectives on whether racism or sexism is present in a particular case? ('I feel offended. So, your comment was offensive. And it concerned race. Hence, it was racist.' Is that good reasoning?)

Epistemic relativism

Are you tempted by the following thinking?

> If a belief is widely accepted within a particular culture, it is well supported within that culture. If people from other cultures do not accept it, then it is not well supported for them. But good support is always a matter of being well supported – actually accepted – by actual people within an actual culture. Thus, the same view might be well supported within one culture and not in another; there would be no culturally independent fact of one of those cultures thereby being correct *and the other one being mistaken.*

That way of thinking is *relativist*. More specifically, it is sometimes called *epistemic* relativism (to distinguish it from relativism about truth, such as we encountered in Chapter 7 (Social constructivism)). The word 'epistemic' refers to knowledge and to standards of support for views. And this relativism implies, for example, that if one cultural group's members believe that everything was created by a special Being (such as a God), then whether they have good support for their belief depends only on whether they meet their own group's accepted standards of support. The fact that most Western scientists would regard that belief about the world's origin as being poorly supported reflects nothing beyond whatever standards of support those scientists happen to accept (say relativists). No culture can be more correct than another about what constitutes good support for a view. Because accepted standards can differ from culture to culture, there is no objectively or independently right standard to apply to a belief – so that even when a view is well supported according to people within one culture (by satisfying their favoured standard), it might not *really* be well supported.

When relativism relies on such claims about cultural groups, it becomes an instance of social constructivism (also introduced in Chapter 7 (Social constructivism)). Specifically, it becomes a social constructivism about standards of support for views. And its succeeding or failing depends on whether there are objective constraints upon good support – constraints applying to all cultural groups. For example, suppose that good support must involve an appropriate link to objective truth – to independent facts. This supposition is widespread among philosophers. And if it is true, might some culturally approved ways of thinking provide only poor support for views? Do some culturally sanctioned ways of thinking fail to lead reliably to objectively true views, even discouraging serious testing of views? Most probably, such ways of thinking would be poor guides to what is objectively true. They might remain culturally significant for the people using them; but a standard's being culturally supported does not ensure its being likely to reveal much that is objectively true of the world. If a given standard's role is mainly ceremonial, perchance (such as by approving of people having views that enhance their fulfilling various social functions), then it possesses cultural worthiness. Again, though, this does not ensure its being a good guide to the world of facts. (Consider the practice of always believing what one's elders or 'social superiors' say. A desire for social cohesion can prevent one's doubting, or disagreeing with, those people. This hardly shows that they are always – or even often – correct.)

A central philosophical distinction underlies these observations. The distinction is sometimes called the *descriptive/evaluative*, or *descriptive/normative*, distinction. And it is as follows. There can be facts as to how people within a culture seek to support their views: 'What standards do they in fact accept?' To answer this is to *describe* what those people *think* are good standards of support. However, we can also ask whether that is how those people *should* seek to support their views, insofar as they want views that *are* true (not only thought to be true): 'Are there more reliable or testable ways of thinking, via which they could know more about the world?' To answer this is to *evaluate* what those people think are good standards of support. It is to ask whether those standards are actually good (not only thought to be good). And (as fallibilism would lead us to expect) no culture is inherently immune to such questioning.

But (contrary to what a relativist would claim) that last concession does not imply that no culture's standards are objectively good guides to what is objectively true. It implies only that we should not assume that *every* culture's standards are good – as good as they need to be, if people within that culture are to be good at gaining true views of the world. (We should always bear in mind how widespread – involving most races in most cultures over many centuries – has been the belief that there is nothing immoral in slavery, for example.) Wherever there is fallibility (which is to say, wherever there are inquirers), there is a possibility of poor standards being used. So, people's satisfying whatever standards are accepted within their culture need not constitute their having good support for their views. Their culture as a whole could be mistaken – even badly so – as to what makes a view well supported. Consequently, relativism about standards is mistaken. Even if people in different cultures do use different standards, this does not imply that none of those standards is poor and that none is good. The previous section explained why agreement among people need not make their views well supported; why would that not remain true when those people are culturally linked to each other? Cultures are fallible, no less so than the people within them. Group solidarity is one thing;

being objectively correct about how best to know the world is quite another. We should not mistake the former for the latter.

Further reading

On good support in general:

Laurence BonJour, *The Structure of Empirical Knowledge* (Cambridge, MA: Harvard University Press, 1985), ch. 1.

Roderick M. Chisholm, *Theory of Knowledge*, 3rd edn (Englewood Cliffs, NJ: Prentice Hall, 1989), ch. 2.

Richard Feldman, *Reason and Argument*, 2nd edn (Upper Saddle River, NJ: Prentice Hall, 1999), ch. 2.

Stephen Cade Hetherington, *Knowledge Puzzles: An Introduction to Epistemology* (Boulder, CO: Westview Press, 1996), ch. 4.

Adam Morton, *A Guide through the Theory of Knowledge*, 3rd edn (Oxford: Blackwell, 2003), chs 1, 5.

Matthias Steup, *An Introduction to Contemporary Epistemology* (Upper Saddle River, NJ: Prentice Hall, 1996), ch. 4.

Richard Swinburne, *Epistemic Justification* (Oxford: Clarendon Press, 2001), chs 1–7.

On reliabilism:

Alvin I. Goldman, *Epistemology and Cognition* (Cambridge, MA: Harvard University Press, 1986), chs 4, 5.

For Popper on testability:

Karl R. Popper, *Conjectures and Refutations: The Growth of Scientific Knowledge*, 4th edn (London: Routledge & Kegan Paul, 1972), ch. 1.

On intellectual virtue:

Linda Trinkaus Zagzebski, *Virtues of the Mind: An Inquiry into the Nature of Virtue and the Ethical Foundations of Knowledge* (Cambridge: Cambridge University Press, 1996).

On epistemic relativism:

Harvey Siegel, *Relativism Refuted: A Critique of Contemporary Epistemological Relativism* (Dordrecht, Holland: D. Reidel, 1987), chs 1, 2, 8.

9

Knowledge

Knowledge's objectivity

Here is one of philosophy's most enduring questions:

> What is it for a view to be knowledge? (What properties must a view have, if it is to be knowledge?)

If we do not know what knowledge is, maybe we fail to know which of our views are knowledge. A view is not knowledge simply by being someone's opinion. Not all confidently held or deeply personal views are knowledge; and being culturally respected does not guarantee a view's being knowledge. Nor is a view knowledge simply because we want it to be, or because we believe or claim that it is. Not all viewpoints are especially knowledgeable. What guarantee do you have of yours being good in that respect?

Probably knowledge's most fundamental property is that of being at least somewhat *objective*. Its presence or absence is not ultimately just a matter of opinion. Someone might say, 'I know what it is that I know. It's my knowledge, after all. If I think that I know something, obviously I do know it.' But if in general that were so, knowing would have no 'worldly' constraints upon it. We would never be answerable, as would-be knowers, to the world beyond ourselves or other people. Yet we are. Knowledge's objectivity is at least that demanding. Knowledge can be present – or absent – even when we do not feel that it is. Knowing is an achievement – and not always one of which we are aware.

Question 9.1 Do only human beings have knowledge? Or do elephants also have it? What about rabbits? Snakes? Slugs? Would all kinds of animals do so? Is having knowledge an essential part of being alive? At any rate, is it essential to living well or meaningfully? Or are only opinions needed for that – regardless of whether they are knowledge? ('He has a view on everything!' Is that good?) Are human beings clearly the best at knowing whatever there is to be known? What would being the best involve?

A traditional conception of knowledge

What makes knowledge objective? The general answer is that it has one or more objective elements, and that there is an objectivity in how it combines its elements. Almost all philosophers regard knowledge as having two objective elements – *truth* (Chapter 7) and *good support* (Chapter 8). How are those elements combined to make knowledge? Here is a generic conception of knowledge:

> Knowing – that is, having a piece of knowledge – is identical to having a true and well supported view.

This form of conception was first discussed in two of Plato's dialogues, the *Meno* and the *Theaetetus*. It has received much subsequent philosophical acceptance. We could call it the *well-supported-true-view* conception of knowledge. (It is a more general version of what is usually termed the *justified-true-belief* conception of knowledge.)

That conception conjoins these two theses:

> *What's-Needed*   If a view is knowledge, then it is true and well supported. (Being true and well supported is *needed* if a view is to be knowledge.)

> *What's-Enough*   If a view is true and well supported, then it is knowledge. (Being true and well supported is *enough* to make a view knowledge.)

There are many ways of instantiating these general theses. What's-Needed implies that if a claim is knowledge, then it is true and (for example) well tested. What's-Enough implies that if a belief is true and (for example) reliably formed, then it is knowledge. ('No, only *conclusively* supported views are knowledge.' In Chapter 12, we consider that suggestion in detail. But first, in the section, Fallible knowledge, I outline what knowledge is like if it requires only good, not perfect, support.)

In a generic way, is the well-supported-true-view conception of knowledge correct? That depends on whether both What's-Needed and What's-Enough are true. The next section to this introduces a philosophically famous, and widely accepted, argument against What's-Enough. In contrast, What's-Needed is almost never questioned. Here is how such a question might arise, though.

Suppose that a correct hunch with which you awoke one morning has led to fruitful investigation. Maybe it appeared to you in a particularly vivid dream. It was an idea that had never previously occurred to you; yet you were mysteriously and unsupportedly confident of its truth.

Was it knowledge – even if puzzlingly so? Presumably you would have preferred to possess good support for it from the start, so that in testing it you were seeking *further* support for it. But it really was a hunch: you began testing without already having support for it. Over time, with testing proceeding, you have rationally strengthened your feeling that the hunch is true. And maybe others agree that what began as a hunch is now knowledge. However, our present question is this: Could your hunch have been knowledge, even before you began testing it? Could it have been some *rare* kind of knowledge, even while lacking the support it would receive later (and after which it becomes a more usual kind of knowledge)? Can knowledge ever be like that? Few epistemologists think so. Consequently, they accept What's-Needed. Are they right to do so?

Question 9.2   When a doctor and I look at an X-ray of part of my body, the doctor gains more knowledge than I do. He or she can see whatever I see there – plus much more, being able to interpret the X-ray accurately. Might there be that kind of disparity between people's capacities – initially? only after education? – as they seek knowledge of the world? For instance, are some people better – and can we improve – at knowing why people act as they do?

Gettier's challenge

These days, few philosophers accept What's-Enough. They hesitate to infer, from a view's being true and well supported, that it is knowledge. This hesitancy is due to a clever article published in 1963 by the American philosopher Edmund Gettier (b. 1927). Epistemologists now assume that if a well supported true view is to be knowledge, the support for it must be either particularly *good*, or some special *kind* of support. How much support would be required? What kind of support is needed? (In Chapter 12 we return to the former question. Until then, our focus is on the latter one.)

Gettier concocted two fanciful yet coherent stories. Each is about someone who forms a belief which is true and well supported. But in each story there is something odd about how that belief is reached. Indeed, so odd is its history that (according to Gettier) the belief fails to be knowledge. And almost all subsequent epistemologists have agreed with him. They have thought of many more ways in which – or so they have argued – this can occur; and they call these possible situations *Gettier cases*. For specificity, here are two quite different Gettier cases (not Gettier's own ones).

The Many   When wandering around your college, you happen upon an area you have not previously visited. (It is behind the building containing the Artificial Intelligence laboratory.) Seeing someone walking nearby, you speak to her. 'What a nice person,' you think, continuing your stroll. And you are correct. But unbeknownst to you, she was the *only* real person around you. Everyone else walking by was a *fake* person – designed by AI researchers, and operated from a nearby room. Your talking to that person was random; you might as easily have approached one of those other beings walking past you. Yet if you had been talking to any of them, you would not have realised that it was not a real person; that is how effective the AI researchers have been. It is mere luck, therefore, that in thinking that you were talking to a person you are correct. You would have had the same thought – albeit mistakenly – if you had been talking to one of those other beings. And it is just good luck that you were not doing that. Hence, although you had a true and well supported belief that you were talking to a person, your belief was not knowledge. At any rate, that is the standard interpretation of cases like this.

The One   Blithely, you continue walking, entering a building. (It contains the AI laboratory.) You amble along a corridor. Stopping outside a room, looking through its doorway, you see what looks like a normal person, reading quietly. Because you are seeking an unoccupied room in which to do some reading yourself, you do not enter. You think, 'There is a person in there. I'll find an empty room.' So, you walk on – unaware that you were seeing a fake person, a cleverly disguised model (one of those by whom you might easily have been fooled in the case of The Many). Never mind, though; your belief was true! There was indeed a person in the room. He was hidden from your sight, meditating. Was your true belief also well supported? Most epistemologists will think so, because you used your senses in a normal way and you reasoned well. (All of this you did in a good-though-fallibilist way.) Yet was your well supported true belief knowledge? Almost no epistemologist would say so.

If that usual initial reaction to Gettier cases is correct, then they challenge the traditional conception of knowledge. They would falsify What's-Enough, by showing that being true and well supported is not always enough to make a view knowledge. Nevertheless (we could still wonder), might *many* views be knowledge simply by being true and well supported? Gettier cases describe quite odd or unusual situations. (Occasionally, they arise in everyday life.) Is being true and well supported *normally* enough to make a view knowledge?

To answer that question, we need to ascertain what makes a situation normal. And this will not be easy. Although philosophers concur that Gettier situations are abnormal, they are yet to agree on *how* such situations are abnormal. What precisely goes wrong in our two Gettier cases? Which aspects of them prevent the well supported true beliefs they contain from being knowledge?

Question 9.3 Is intellectual conformity – thinking like most other people – required for knowledge? 'Of course not,' you might reply, 'I get *my* knowledge in *my* way.' If you think in unusual ways, though, won't others find it hard to agree that you have knowledge? Could you have it anyway? Is being imaginative more – or is it less – likely to give someone knowledge? Do others ever mistake someone's being imaginative for his or her thinking poorly? (Would hallucinogenic drugs 'open the doors to knowledge of a deeper reality'? Or would they undermine one's chances of gaining much knowledge? Do they spark knowledgeable creativity? Or do they squash both knowledge and creativity?)

Avoiding false evidence

There have been many attempts to find an analysis of knowledge that explains why, in Gettier cases, there is a lack of knowledge. In this section, I present one simple attempt. It begins with a thesis like this:

> If your support for a view relies upon some false evidence, then the view is not knowledge. So long as your good support for a true view relies upon no false evidence, that view is knowledge.

In the case of The Many, for instance (according to this suggestion), the reason why your belief that you were talking to a person fails to be knowledge is that your support for that belief relies, in part, upon your false belief that all the beings around you are people. Without this belief, you would have become cautious – to say the least – about thinking that you were talking to a person. Once some falsity enters your thinking, therefore, does all knowledge depart? And is knowledge present, other things being equal, if all of your evidence is true?

Most epistemologists will not think so, probably because there might even be Gettier cases in which no false evidence is relied upon. (This idea comes from an article by an American philosopher, Richard Feldman: b. 1948.) In the case of The One, it seems, you reasoned like this:

> That's a person. So, there is a person in that room.

The first of those two thoughts is your evidence – and it is false. But imagine altering that case slightly, so that you reason in this way instead:

> That looks like a person. (And whatever looks like a person is almost certainly a person.) So, there is a person in that room.

Now you would be relying on no false evidence: Even though the being whom you see is not a person, he *does* look like one, and whatever looks like a person *is* almost certainly one. Accordingly, in this variation on the original case of The One, you use only true beliefs as evidence from which to infer your true conclusion – which continues to be the belief that there is a person in the room. Your support for this belief is, as before, good-though-fallibilist. So, you have a true and well supported belief this time, relying upon no false evidence. Yet if your final belief in the case's original version was not knowledge, presumably it still fails to be knowledge of there being a person in that room. So (it will be said), even using good evidence, all of which is true, is not enough to make a true view knowledge. What *is* enough, then?

Question 9.4 Do some people possess higher self-esteem than is objectively warranted (because they have many more failings than they admit to themselves)? Is this in itself a reason why these people should have even *lower* self-esteem? Is it possible to have high self-esteem without knowing much about one's character and capacities? Is self-belief distinct from self-knowledge? What is self-knowledge knowledge *of*? Is it knowledge of one's abilities and tendencies, one's strengths and weaknesses? How can people obtain this knowledge? Many of us do not always want self-knowledge, it seems – preferring a self-belief that flatters rather than reveals. Why might that be so? Can self-knowledge improve one's character – even when not being 'psychologically affirming'?

Knowing luckily

Post-1963 philosophy has produced no consensus on what knowledge is, or on how to justify the standard interpretation of Gettier cases as being situations from which knowledge is absent. Maybe we should try thinking non-standardly about the nature of knowledge. Might the usual interpretation of Gettier cases be incorrect? Might such cases be situations in which a person *has* the knowledge being denied to him or her by the standard interpretation?

Let's reflect on the *luck* operating within Gettier cases. In the case of The Many, you had a well supported true belief that you were talking to a person. Yet the fake people were so life-like that if you had been speaking instead to one of them, you would still have believed that you were talking to a person. Hence, even while having seemingly the same sort of evidence (an experience of talking to someone near that AI building), you could easily have formed a false belief (the same belief, but this time reacting to a fake person). So, according to the standard interpretation, your well supported true belief is not knowledge – because the good support has led to a true belief too luckily. But here is an alternative interpretation of that case:

> Why can't knowing sometimes involve such luck? You have the knowledge – the well supported true belief that you were talking to a person – *because* of some

luck. Most luck in such a situation would deprive you of knowledge – because it would be bad luck (with your talking to a fake person having been more likely). The luck on this occasion happened to be good luck – giving you the knowledge. (A belief can be knowledge without your realising how luckily it is knowledge.)

The case of The One can be interpreted similarly. Looking through the door, you saw what you did not know was a fake person. Quite reasonably, you inferred that there was a person in the room. Being fallibilist (in Chapter 8's (Fallibilism) sense), your observational evidence could have led to a false belief – as it would have done in this case, had there not luckily been a person elsewhere in the room, hidden from your gaze. In almost all situations, you would be unlucky to infer a *false* belief that there is a person in a given room, upon seeing what looks exactly like a person inside it. In this case, you were lucky to infer, from that same observational evidence, the *true* belief that there is a person in the room. You might easily not have come to know that there was a person in the room. You were lucky to do so. Why can't knowing sometimes be like that?

Such knowledge is not ideal, of course. If you were to find out how you gained your well supported true belief in this case, you would be surprised. But does this imply that your well supported true belief was not knowledge? Can you ever know something in a way that would surprise you, if you were to find out that this was how you reached your view? Or must you have formed your view more normally and predictably – so that you would not be surprised, if you were to find out how you reached your view? Must knowledge be gained in some standard way? Or could it be gained quite luckily? And if it can ever be so luckily present, then maybe whatever luck is present in Gettier cases does not force us, after all, to reject What's-Enough. We could continue thinking that all true and well supported views are instances of knowledge. We need only acknowledge that sometimes such knowledge is present rather luckily, even without our realising how lucky we have been to gain it.

Question 9.5 Imagine hiring one of two equally qualified people – a black woman, a white man. Perhaps you are confident that you will be acting more ethically if you hire the black woman (in accordance with a well-meant policy of affirmative action). But what if this man has suffered great prejudice and other hardship in his life, whereas this woman has led a life of comfort and privilege? If you were to know these facts, would you hire the man instead? In practice, you would probably not know those further facts. Would you need do so, though, if you were to act as ethically as possible? Given those facts, would hiring the woman be the less ethical choice on this occasion? (Does thinking that one is being more ethical not guarantee one's being more ethical?) Unfortunately, could acting ethically sometimes require a person to have knowledge beyond what he or she has, or indeed will ever have?

Gradualism

The previous section's idea – that sometimes knowing a fact involves quite a lot of luck – might suggest this thesis:

> A fact can be known more or less well.

In general, to know a fact in a normal way is to know it in a way that is fairly solid and secure, maybe well tested, reasonably reliably formed. To know a fact more luckily is to know it in a way that is less solid and secure, probably poorly tested, not so reliably formed. And usually it is preferable to know a fact more, rather than less, solidly and securely – having a better tested, or more reliably formed, true view. This would be *better* knowledge of the fact in question. It need not be more useful or significant knowledge. But if you wish to know whether there is a person in a specific room, for example, you gain better knowledge of there being one there, if you gain the knowledge in a normal way – with the room being normal, for a start. You gain dramatically poorer knowledge that there is a person there, if you gain it as luckily as in our Gettier case of The One. (When philosophers think that being in a Gettier situation deprives one of knowledge, might they be mistaking knowing a fact very poorly for lacking that knowledge?)

There are further applications of that way of thinking about knowledge. Can a particular fact be known better by one person than by another? I might know better than you do that kangaroos routinely hop. And can a fact be known better by someone at one time than at another? Maybe I know better now than when I was a child that kangaroos routinely hop.

Here is how there could be such variations in the quality of knowledge of a particular fact:

> Someone's true view is better or worse knowledge of a particular fact, in accordance with the quality of his or her *support* for that view. (With the knowledge including the support, the support's being better or worse makes the knowledge better or worse.)

This is a *gradualist* conception of knowledge, because it says that there can be grades of knowledge, even grades of knowledge of the one fact. It does not conflict with knowledge's objectivity. Knowledge can remain knowledge of facts (in Chapter 7's (Correspondence) sense). Moreover, whatever support the knowledge includes is objectively better or worse (in Chapter 8's sense).

The gradualist conception denies, however, that knowledge is *absolute*. Just as support for a view can be objectively good without being absolute (Chapter 8 (Fallibilism)), the same is true of knowledge whenever it *includes* such support. For instance, maybe in a normal situation, thinking in an everyday way, you know fairly well that you are a person. But possibly in a philosophy class you think unusually hard about what it is to be a person – trying to answer the questions in Chapter 1! Hopefully, you improve your understanding of what persons are, strictly speaking. Might this result in your knowing better within the philosophy class than within the more normal context that you are a person? Gradualism accepts that this is indeed possible. There can be different ways of knowing a particular fact; equally, there could be different qualities – different grades – of knowledge of that fact. Gradualism is inclusive in this respect.

Question 9.6   How good is the following reasoning? 'Everyone knows extremely well that each pregnant woman is a person; realistically, we could not know this better than we do. Yet even if each foetus is actually a person, no one's knowledge of this could be quite so good; there is too much controversy and uncertainty among well-intentioned people on this issue. If a decision must be made regarding whether to allow a particular foetus to be aborted, stronger knowledge should be favoured over what is at best weaker knowledge. We know better that a woman is a person than we could know that a foetus is a person. Hence, we should allow the pregnant woman to choose whether to have an abortion.'

Fallible knowledge

Gradualism supports the idea of there being fallible knowledge. For fallible knowledge of a fact is not the *best possible* knowledge of that fact. It is knowledge in which the support is not perfect or conclusive – better than it might have been, although not as good as is possible.

For example, you might know that you want to eat dinner soon, without having conclusive or infallibilist support for your belief that you have that desire. You have good support for your belief by being aware of a feeling which you interpret – accurately – as a desire for dinner. But you could have misinterpreted your feeling, by thinking that it was a pang of love, say. Consequently, you might have lacked the knowledge which in fact you have of wanting to eat dinner. You thereby possess this knowledge fallibly. (Infallible knowledge would require support which is incapable of leading you astray. You would *inevitably* form a correct view on the basis of it. You have such knowledge rarely – if ever.)

Accordingly, we need to understand the nature of fallible knowledge. Aren't we fallible creatures with fallible minds, sometimes lacking knowledge we think we have? And many people, when reminded of these limitations, react thus: 'Then we never have knowledge, because we cannot escape our fallibility.' Yet that reaction might be premature (as I will explain more fully in Chapter 12 (Knowing fallibly)). If being unable to escape our fallibility means that all of our views are mistaken, then indeed we never have knowledge. (A mistaken view is false – and therefore not knowledge.) But being unable to escape our fallibility might often be, instead, our gaining knowledge *in a fallibilist way*. This would be our knowing various facts in ways that *might not* have led to our having those pieces of knowledge. It would be our knowing those facts in ways that are not providing the *best possible* knowledge of them.

Most contemporary epistemologists are fallibilists about knowledge in something like that way. They would urge us, when claiming knowledge, to do so with humility – conscious that our support for our views could have led us astray, even if thankfully it has not done so on a particular occasion. Our good-though-fallibilist support for our views, even when it has led us to views which are true, might not have done so. Even when we know something, therefore, is there a touch of good fortune in our doing so?

Question 9.7 'The success in my life has always felt predestined. I was *meant* to be a champion. I had talent. I never shirked hard work.' But isn't luck needed at each moment of one's life? Can one know infallibly that one will be successful in life? Can one know infallibly why one has been successful? Is it possible to mistake fallible knowledge for infallible knowledge? Is it possible to mistake a lack of knowledge for infallible knowledge?

Education

Does gradualism about knowledge make sense of the following puzzling phenomenon? In an introductory class at university, you should become familiar with some significant truths. You listen; you learn; you know. 'What's next?' you might ask. Yet when you enrol in a more advanced class on that subject, you could find the teacher discussing, in part, the *same* significant truths as you thought you already knew from the introductory class. (Certainly in philosophy classes this can occur.) 'Why? I know these. I learnt them last year.' Of course, you are probably being presented with new *support* for those truths – more detailed explanations, conceptual refinements. But if you already know these truths, you do not need new support for them – at least not so that in the advanced class you finally know them. Yes, you gain further knowledge, related knowledge, which you might find independently interesting. However, *this* outcome could also be achieved by the teacher's introducing wholly new topics, taking the old knowledge for granted. Is there any special point to revisiting the old knowledge?

There can be – if gradualism is correct. If knowledge of a fact can be better or worse, possibly it can be *improved* over time. Knowledge gained in the introductory class could, in the advanced class, become better knowledge of those same facts. We often talk of deepening our knowledge of some fact. This is how that can happen. And only the gradualist conception accommodates this way of talking, rendering it literally true. To deepen your knowledge of a fact is in part to improve your knowledge of it; what you learn in an advanced class might well improve the knowledge you gained in the introductory class. This would occur by improving your support for those truths you have already learned.

Accordingly, a gradualist conception of knowledge reveals part of the point of a good education. Not only can we, via education, gain knowledge of facts; continued education might improve our knowledge of them.

Question 9.8   Does your knowledge – what you know, how you know, how well you know – always reflect your social or economic class, your gender, your racial properties (and more)? Do males and females, for instance, tend to know in different ways? (In which ways would we know this?) Might some such ways be *better* than others for gaining various kinds of knowledge? Might some aspects of the world generally be known better by males, or by females? If this is so, need it be so? Can knowledge of some aspects of reality be heightened by social deprivation? Can knowledge of some aspects of reality be blunted by social deprivation?

Taking knowledge seriously

There are dangers, both conceptual and political, in not taking knowledge seriously. We should be especially careful not to talk or think about knowledge in ways that overlook or belittle its objectivity. This can occur when people become social constructivists about truth (Chapter 7 (Social constructivism)) or relativists about standards for good support (Chapter 8 (Epistemic relativism)). We have already seen why those are misleading ideas about truth and support.

How else might people talk or think as if knowledge is not objective? One widespread 'technique' is to use quotation-marks inappropriately. For instance, people start speaking of 'knowledge', not knowledge. (Often they wave fingers in the air to indicate those quotation-marks.) A related 'technique' is to replace talk of knowledge with talk of knowledge-claims. (Sometimes – awkwardly – these are called knowledges.) Anyone can *claim* knowledge of anything – irrespective of whether they really possess the knowledge being claimed. So, when we treat the claiming of knowledge as tantamount to the having of knowledge, we devalue the significance of knowing. I have heard respected academics talk like this: 'Even if it didn't happen as they claimed, they still have their "knowledges" – which must be respected as valid.' This just says that even if the views in question are false, we should (for some personal or social reason) ignore that falsity, acting as if the views are really knowledge. By all means, do this to be nice; do not mistake it for being accurate or insightful, though.

Imagine saying – without having done supporting research – to an Amnesty International representative that he or she only 'knows' that suffering is occurring in country Y. (And let your fingers portray those quotation-marks.) Whether intentionally or not, you would be *denying* – and not on the basis of competing research – that the representative knows of any suffering happening in Y. Wouldn't you therefore be treating in a cavalier and disrespectful way the potential reality of suffering occurring within Y? We trivialise the achievement that is knowledge if we neglect real differences such as those between knowledge and opinion, between knowing and claiming, and between knowing and having a view. To diminish knowledge's nature can be to demean real plights, genuine quests for justice.

Sometimes, when people devalue knowledge, they do so for political purposes which they think *aid* quests for justice. But even a worthy political aim can be undermined if one misunderstands the nature of knowledge. Suppose you believe that knowledge is a mere instrument of power, a political implement – nothing more. Your support for this view might be the accurate observation that powerful or privileged people (in many societies, tribal and non-tribal alike) often restrict others' access to knowledge, elevating their own views to the status of a culture's 'official' knowledge. Various institutions (such as governments and religions) might abet this oppression, teaching less privileged people not to feel that they are unfairly being deprived of knowledge. However, telling these people that there is no real knowledge, and that their 'knowledge' (their 'voice') is all they need, merely perpetuates that oppression. (Note those feminists who urge women not to seek scientific knowledge – 'men's knowledge'.) Scorning knowledge in principle, such as by routinely referring to 'knowledge' rather than knowledge, hardly lessens knowledge's reality and potency. At best, it makes those with less access to knowledge feel better about their lack of it. For many purposes in life, though, people need knowledge, not 'knowledge'. Even if they are unaware of this, their lives could be improved by gaining real knowledge instead of settling for having 'knowledge' and making knowledge-claims. They might even need good knowledge of significant facts. Although the right to make knowledge-claims is a non-trivial political right to a form of free speech, it includes no guarantee of that speech voicing real understanding, real knowledge. When powerful people stunt others' chances of gaining beneficial knowledge, this is an abuse of power. Yet we help no one – other than the abusers – by inferring that having knowledge is not, after all, important. Instead, we should critically examine whether those in power have the knowledge they claim to have. We cannot do this if we talk as though there is *no* knowledge, or (conversely) if we let *all* beliefs or claims amount to knowledge.

The concept of knowledge is not political in itself; it has no political component. But we have found reasons for thinking that it has these three fundamental properties:

> Knowledge is *objective* (Knowledge's objectivity section) and *graded* (Gradualism section) and *fallible* (Fallible knowledge section). (Objectivity and fallibility are commonly attributed to knowledge; viewing it as gradational is non-standard.)

No one, no matter how powerful or privileged, can make himself or herself a knower – let alone an infallible knower – on some occasion by deciding or decreeing that he or she is one. And whatever those with power and privilege do know might not be known so well by them. We are thus always philosophically entitled to question whether those with power and privilege have knowledge they claim to have.

This point also applies more broadly, to whatever is cultural in general, not only whatever is narrowly political. Knowledge's objectivity implies that even views which are entrenched – powerful, privileged – within a *culture* might not be knowledge. A view could be culturally supported by being traditional within a group, perhaps by not upsetting the group's solidarity or social harmony. Yet often this is no indicator of the claim's being likely to be true. (Think of how a family can 'close ranks' behind a family member, rejecting serious inquiry into the truth of accusations against him or her: 'He's a good boy. I won't hear anything bad said about him.') Crucially, it seems, not all cultures *value* quests for truth that could result in their established views being found not to be knowledge. (Are religious cultures like that? What of those academic cultures within which intellectual fashions exert great sway? What of those that scorn clarity while forever claiming profundity?)

Famously, Popper distinguished between *open* societies and *closed* ones. A society that is closed on a given topic does not respect a fully questioning search for well supported true views on that topic, preferring the cultural solidarity of traditional views. That society is not open to the possibility of its received wisdom on that topic being found to be false. That received 'wisdom' is therefore never *tested* (in the Popperian sense outlined in Chapter 8 (Popper and testability)). Might such 'wisdom' rarely be wisdom?

This failing could be present within any given culture or society. Nevertheless, this is not to say that it *is* present within all cultures or societies, or that it is present to equal degrees within all cultures or societies. How open are those around you to testing their more cherished views? Should we seek knowledge by courting the real possibility of finding that we lack it? Will you never have much knowledge, let alone much good knowledge of deep or provocative facts, if you are not open to that daring possibility? (Yet once we do take such a possibility seriously, will we *lose* too much knowledge? Will doubt run rampant? Chapter 12 suggests an optimistic answer to these questions.)

Further reading

On the well-supported-true-view conception of knowledge:

Robert Audi, *Epistemology: A Contemporary Introduction to the Theory of Knowledge* (London: Routledge, 1998), ch. 8.

A.J. Ayer, *The Problem of Knowledge* (London: Macmillan, 1956), ch. 1.

Colin Radford, *Driving to California: An Unconventional Introduction to Philosophy* (Edinburgh: Edinburgh University Press, 1996), Part 2, ch. 1.

On Gettier's challenge and responses to it:

Stephen Cade Hetherington, *Knowledge Puzzles: An Introduction to Epistemology* (Boulder, CO: Westview Press, 1996), chs 5–11, 14–17.

Adam Morton, *A Guide through the Theory of Knowledge*, 3rd edn (Oxford: Blackwell, 2003), ch. 6.

Paul K. Moser (ed.), *Empirical Knowledge: Readings in Contemporary Epistemology* (Totowa, NJ: Rowman & Littlefield, 1986), Part II. (This book contains the articles by Gettier and Feldman referred to in the sections, Gettier's challenge and Avoiding false evidence.)

Robert K. Shope, *The Analysis of Knowing: A Decade of Research* (Princeton, NJ: Princeton University Press, 1983).

Richard Swinburne, *Epistemic Justification* (Oxford: Clarendon Press, 2001), ch. 8.

On gradualism about knowledge:

Stephen Hetherington, *Good Knowledge, Bad Knowledge: On Two Dogmas of Epistemology* (Oxford: Clarendon Press, 2001).

On not taking knowledge seriously:

Roger Sandall, *The Culture Cult: Designer Tribalism and Other Essays* (Boulder, CO: Westview Press, 2001).

David Stove, *Popper and After: Four Modern Irrationalists* (Oxford: Pergamon Press, 1982), Part 1.

For Popper on open, and on closed, societies:

K.R. Popper, *The Open Society and its Enemies*, vol. I, 5th edn (London: Routledge & Kegan Paul, 1966), ch. 10.

Observational Knowledge

Purely observational knowledge

Chapter 9 described in a general way what knowledge is. We can characterise it more fully by finding out from where our knowledge ultimately *comes*. What are the most fundamental sources of your knowledge? Are your friends that authoritative? No. What of your teachers? Again, no. Your society? Alas, no. Deeper sources underwrite those ones. Historically, philosophy has thought mainly about these two – *observation* (looking, listening, and so on) and *reason* (inferring, thinking through implications, pure rational insight). Is it because you sense the world, and because you have insights of reason, that you have knowledge at all?

This chapter asks what contributions your powers of observation can make to your having knowledge. Even if you could observe everything observable, would there remain limits to what you know? How far can your sensory powers take you towards knowing whatever there is to be known? This chapter is about observation *as such* – pure observation. Is there any purely observational knowledge? Imagine a machine having always deprived you of all intellect, all capacity to reason – leaving you only your senses. Could you nonetheless have gained some knowledge? (Chapter 11 asks the analogous question about *reason's* possible contribution to knowledge. Then, in Chapter 12, we consider ways in which philosophers have questioned whether even observation *plus* reason can give us knowledge.)

Question 10.1 Could a computer ever be *wise*? Input; output; wisdom? Is it possible for people to be wise if they only ever observe, without ever reflecting? That is, are some sorts of experience sufficient for wisdom? Are some kinds of experience at least necessary for wisdom? Do some forms of experience *lessen* one's chances of gaining wisdom? (Would prolonged exposure to computer games do so? What of contemporary music videos? What of violent movies? If these kinds of experience are to coexist with having some wisdom, must they be counteracted by one's also having other experiences? Which ones?)

Observational limits?

Are there views which appear to be purely observational – but which are not? Are the views discussed in the following cases like that? Maybe limits exist to how much support our senses as such can provide for some views.

Stick in water   'Bend' a formerly straight stick by immersing part of it in water! Amaze your (less thoughtful) friends; impress (gullible) strangers. You believe that the stick is not really bent; nevertheless, it looks bent. So, is pure observation failing to let you know that the stick is not bent? ('No. Although the stick looks bent, it doesn't *feel* bent.' Yet might your intellect, not your senses, be telling you which of those 'competing' observations to favour?)

Descartes's beeswax   In his *Meditation II*, Descartes pondered a piece of wax. He observed it closely – how it looked, smelt, tasted, and so on. But as he approached the heat of his fireplace, those sensory qualities were replaced by different ones. The wax softened, losing its former aroma and taste, and so on. Was it still numerically the same piece of wax as before? Of course it was (thought Descartes). Yet how could he know this? He believed that he could do so only via his reason, his pure intellect – not his senses. The senses provided first one group of observations, then a second group. This was all that they could do.

Personal identity   How can you know that someone who was a friend of yours when you were ten years old is the same person as someone who is a friend of yours now? The observable qualitative changes have been dramatic. Do you literally observe a single entity persisting despite those changes? Or can you know of the person's persistence only through some wholly or partly non-observational means? ('I've seen my friend many times over the years. I've observed a single entity surviving that multitude of small changes.' But did you really observe the single entity? Or did you observe first one group of qualities, then a new one, then another, and so on – a slightly different group each time?)

Induction   You touch a frog; it jumps. You touch it again; it jumps once more. You are about to touch it for a third time. Do you know that it will jump on this occasion? That would be inductive knowledge. You would be reasoning from what you have observed, to a view about what you have not yet observed (perhaps because it is yet to occur). Would such reasoning therefore take you beyond your observations, strictly speaking? You have not experienced what the frog will do on this next occasion; you only have experiential evidence of what *has* occurred (including, maybe, other people's observations of frogs). Consequently, if you can know that the frog will jump, is this knowledge partly non-observational? Does it involve your pure intellect somehow transcending your senses? (We return to this sort of case in Chapter 12 (Hume on induction).)

Testimony If you are to know much about the world, presumably you need to rely greatly on what other people tell you. How do you know that the earth orbits the sun? You have encountered the testimony of others to that effect. Did you take for granted their generally being sincere and trustworthy? If so, were you going beyond what you could observe? ('No, I have observed people being sincere and trustworthy on other occasions. So, I know – I'm not simply assuming – that people are generally to be believed.' Does this kind of response return us to Induction, above? Are you resorting to inductive reasoning – hence still going beyond observation – about others' trustworthiness?)

Other minds Do you really observe other people being in pain? After all, you do not feel their feelings. You observe their wincing and crying, their saying that they are in pain. But if none of this is their actual pain, must you *infer* – relying on something beyond what you observe – that they are in pain, if you are to know that they are? (Chapter 12 (Other minds) pursues this question.)

Moral wrongness Perhaps you can observe people being attacked, followed by their behaving as if in pain. Do you also observe the attack's moral wrongness? Is this an observable property – 'out there' in the world? Where, exactly, is it? (Or is it, for example, a reaction within you, such as a feeling of pity? Then could you observe the wrongness by having that feeling?)

Question 10.2 If you could only observe, not reason, would you never know that there are people around you? 'I see someone over there.' 'No, you don't. A person has a front and a back. You can see only a back! You have to *infer* or *reason* that there is also a front over there.' Are people more real – or are they less so – if you can know them only in this way?

Empiricism

If you believe that ultimately all knowledge is observational, you are an *empiricist*. This philosophical stance began being developed fully in the seventeenth and eighteenth centuries, especially in Britain. Its three best-known exponents were Locke, the Irish Bishop George Berkeley (1685–1753), and Hume. It began as a kind of view about our concepts or ideas. These are the sources and elements of knowledge. So, these days, empiricism's basic thesis is presented in this way:

> All knowledge is empirical knowledge. That is, ultimately it is observational – because, when all is said and done, good support for a view is always observational. (Until you observe the world, you know nothing.)

(Empiricism also allows you to reason. However, it requires you to be using principles that you can support observationally – as in, for instance, 'This is a good way to reason, because most people reason like this.' That is why I used the word 'ultimately' in formulating empiricism.)

It is possible to be selectively empiricist. For instance, you might be an empiricist about morality and not about mathematics. If you believe that all knowledge of whether a particular action is morally right depends only upon observing what happens when people act like that ('Does it inflict pain upon people?'), you are thinking empirically about morality. On the other hand, if you believe that numbers are unobservable, yet that we can know much about them, you are a Platonist, not an empiricist, about numbers.

Empiricism is science's 'official' generic outlook. Indeed, empiricism historically arose as science prospered: with people observing the world more scientifically, they seemed to know it more fully. Yet much is described in science that is not strictly observable; who has ever directly observed a quark? And scientists often reason in ways that are not clearly observational: highly abstract mathematics is at the heart of much science. Has even science therefore not always been purely empirical? Does it not rely wholly upon observation in supporting its claims?

Similar questions arise about the social sciences. For instance, do we know empirically that intellectual abilities are distributed fairly evenly around the world, among people from different cultures and with different racial lineages? Or can this be known without detailed empirical investigation? (Some people find such questions offensive. But might it be the uses to which some people would put various possible answers that should seem offensive?)

Are there views that need more empirical support than might be realised? Many politicians, it seems, are perpetually scared of 'sending the wrong message' about crime, drugs, sex education, and so on. This usually leads to their trying to enact 'law and order' legislation, encoding stricter punishments, less medical intervention, more police powers. However, what if the best available empirical research were to conclude that crime and dangerous drug use would decrease, and that there would be fewer unwanted pregnancies among unmarried teenagers, if a less punitive legislative approach were to be implemented? So many people 'Just Know What Is To Be Done' – in spite of never having consulted or performed serious empirical research. Sometimes a religious doctrine tells them how to approach these issues. In any case, they say, 'The last thing we want to do as a society is to send the message that we are condoning such behaviour. This would only encourage our young people to indulge in it.' But *if* these are empirical issues, should political policy respect that empirical evidence – even if that evidence supports a less punitive policy? (And I write this as someone who has never sampled cigarettes or illegal drugs, or tasted beer, spirits, wine, and so on. I might be thought to be someone who would advocate only increased punishment in these matters, wherever punishment is appropriate at all. Philosophically, though, these issues are not so simple. We must respect good observational evidence – wherever it leads.)

Is empiricism part of the 'official' underlying philosophy of contemporary Western cultures? ('We learn by observing. If a view cannot be well supported by observation, it is irrational.') Yet many people, it seems, wish to gain insights – knowledge – transcending observation. Whether that is possible depends upon the nature and power of observation. What (we should wonder) *is* perception?

Question 10.3 'Of course I'm a good person. I know that I am.' Would you make this claim about yourself? Would you be making an *empirical* claim? Are you genuinely open to the possibility of conceding, on the basis of good observational evidence, that you are not a good person? Or is your belief that you are a good person more a piece of personal faith than an empirically testable claim? (Is it self-belief, not self-knowledge?) Would you always dismiss, as seriously flawed, any supposed empirical evidence of your not being good? Is everyone a good person – 'really, in his or her own way'?

Representationalism

There are several philosophical theories of what it is to observe or perceive the world. According to *direct* (or *naive*) *realism*, for example, whenever you perceive something, you directly perceive the thing itself. Here you are, watching a cat; there it is, purring; and you are directly aware of it, courtesy of your eyes. 'I see the cat – itself, directly.' What could be simpler?

But direct realism has often been questioned by philosophers, especially those holding a *representational* theory of perception. (Locke was one such representationalist.) When you observe a cat, is there a picture – more generally, a representation – of it in your mind? A representationalist says that there is. Not only is there you and the cat; there is also – literally, as a further entity – a representation-in-your-mind-of-the-cat. And what you *directly* perceive is the idea as such – not the cat as such. How could that be so?

Representationalism gained philosophical popularity when scientific developments revealed perception's causal complexity – its *indirectness* in revealing the world. Sometimes representationalism looks to *the argument from illusion*. Recall your 'feat' (in the section, Observational limits?) of 'bending' a stick in water. That is a sensory illusion, because the stick looks – but is not actually – bent. So, the immediate object of your awareness is not the actual stick. It is the 'its-looking-to-you-as-if-the-stick-is-bent'. It is an experienced *appearance* (representationalists also use the terms *idea* and *sense-datum*) of a bent stick. You are directly aware of having this experience or idea. Of course, it is an illusory – inaccurate, non-veridical – experience. But purely 'from within' (without resorting to *reasoning* about how accurate your respective sensory ideas are), you need not experience any difference between illusory and non-illusory ideas. In each case, there is a mental experience, which might – or might not – be accurate, veridical. Representationalism concludes that you perceive the 'outer' world only indirectly: your direct perception is *always* of an 'inner' idea or experience whose content apparently represents some state of affairs outside you.

That representationalist picture of perception has been philosophically influential. It has worried many philosophers – because, as the early empiricists realised with some concern, it raises the possibility of our never *knowing* whether we are really perceiving the world around us. If perception is inherently indirect, with there being no intrinsic, purely observational, difference between accurate ideas and illusory ones, might we lack all observational knowledge of the world? How can you know – 'from within' – whether your apparent observations are revealing the world accurately? Are you restricted to understanding accurately your own ideas – and *not* thereby the 'outside' world?

Admittedly, we often label particular experiences as being non-illusory. ('If we had no veridical experiences, we couldn't call others illusions. The word "illusion" would be useless.') Yet perhaps we are never correct in calling some experiences non-illusory. And even if we are, possibly we never know which ones are accurate. So, might we continually and inadvertently deceive ourselves as to how well, if at all, we perceive a real world 'out there'? We return to these questions in Chapter 12. Let's first consider (in the next section) their metaphysical dimension: Need a real world, 'out there', even *exist*? Or might there be no such world for us ever to know? We have ideas which we almost always think reflect a real world outside our minds; maybe no such world exists, though. Could our ideas represent without reflecting?

Question 10.4   Can no man know what it is like to be a woman? 'Yes. No man senses the world as a woman does.' Does no woman know what it is like to be a man? 'Yes. No woman senses the world as a man does.' Must people never know what it is like to be from cultural or racial groups other than their own? 'Yes. They never sense the world as members of other such groups.' But if no one can ever transcend his or her gender or racial ancestry in these ways, how much cognitive point is there to hearing others *tell* us what it is like to be them? How well can any-one understand what others tell them about what it is to live as those others do?

Berkeley's idealism

Berkeley's empiricism reached a highly distinctive verdict on the nature of the physical world. Like representationalists, Berkeley assumed that we perceive physical objects by being directly aware of ideas in our minds. But, unlike representationalists, he thought that we perceive objects directly. This is because (argued Berkeley) physical objects *are* ideas in minds. Here is the essence of his reasoning for that bold claim:

> We know the physical world observationally. Hence, it is knowable by us only insofar as we know it-as-it-appears-to-us. So, *what* we know, in knowing the world, is it-as-it-appears-to-us. Accordingly, the world *is* the world-as-observed.

For example, being a table is nothing more than being observed to be that table. We have no empirical – no strictly observational – grounds for thinking that being a table is anything more than that. We cannot observe it as it is not observed. Hence, our evidence as to what is observed – namely, the table as observed – is not evidence of the table's existing *without* being observed.

Yet, as Berkeley acknowledged, we do not always observe all objects. Does the table cease existing whenever no one observes it? As far as I am aware, no one thinks that it does. Even Berkeley did not think so. But how could he reconcile this standard belief in the table's continued, although unobserved, existence with his central claim that physical objects exist only by being perceived?

Berkeley's most discussed attempt at that reconciliation took this form:

> The table persists as an idea in God's mind, even when it is not in any of our minds. (God's is an infinite mind, unlike any of ours.) When we are not perceiving the table, God still has in mind an idea of it.

Thus we have the core of Berkeley's metaphysics, grounded in his empiricist epistemology:

There are minds – one infinite, many finite – with ideas. Many of those ideas are of physical objects. Those objects *are* those ideas. The physical is thus mental. (A specific table is an idea of that table.)

Unsurprisingly, therefore, Berkeley's theory is standardly called an *idealism* – in the sense of an *idea-ism* – about the physical world. It is also termed an *immaterialism*: he is denying that the world contains physical matter, or substance, which could exist even if never observed. (Locke had argued that the world does indeed encompass such matter, although he admitted that in itself it would be '*something*, ... we know not what'.)

Famously, Berkeley's idealism gave rise to a pair of limericks. The first was by Ronald Knox:

There once was a man who said: 'God
Must think it exceedingly odd
    If he finds that this tree
    Continues to be
When there's no one about in the Quad.'

Then this reply (by 'Anon.') appeared, in the spirit of Berkeley's theory:

Dear Sir, Your astonishment's odd:
I am always about in the Quad,
    And that's why the tree
    Will continue to be,
Since observed by Yours faithfully, God.

Serious objections, too, have been made against Berkeleian idealism. Here is one:

Even if (as empiricists claim) an object is only ever known observationally, this does not entail that (as Berkeley also claims) the object is *only* as it is known observationally. We cannot know observationally that it has no further features beyond observed ones. In order to do so, we would have to know observationally what the object is like *beyond* how we observationally know it to be. And of course we cannot do that.

This does not prove that an object has features beyond those that are known observationally. But how could Berkeley know – observationally – that there are none (concludes the objection)?

Question 10.5 Do different people always see a table differently? Do they therefore see different tables? (By seeing reality differently, do different people see wholly disparate realities?) Instead of a single table, are there as many tables as there are people with ideas of a table there? Should different people never use the same *word* as each other in describing what they observe? ('There is a shared table, observed by all. It is the *collection* of the many individual ideas of it.' So, in seeing the table, am I seeing a collection of ideas, including other people's ideas? How on earth could I do that?)

Phenomenalism

Almost no contemporary philosophers are Berkeleian idealists about the physical world. But some have adopted a variation on Berkeley's famous reasoning. They are called *phenomenalists*. Roughly, phenomenalism is Berkeley's-idealism-as-modified-so-as-not-to-be-positing-God. (Berkeley himself saw the possibility of this kind of analysis.)

Phenomenalism tells us that a table, for example, is not only the ideas we have in observing it. The table is also whatever ideas we *would* experience if we were to be observing it when, in fact, we are not doing so. Presumably, the 'table observations' you do experience are sufficiently similar to those you would experience. Berkeley said that when we do not observe the table, God remains aware of it; phenomenalism says that even when we are not observing the table, we could be doing so – and if we were to do so, we would have similar experiences to those we have when actually observing it. The table is thus a blend of actual and possible observations of it. (The English phenomenalist John Stuart Mill (1806–73) called physical objects 'permanent possibilities of sensation'.) Physical reality is as it is, and as it would be, represented in our minds; and it would not exist, were our minds never to have such ideas. We create physical reality – by the power of our minds.

Phenomenalism aims to be an empiricist theory, basing all knowledge upon observations. Does it succeed in that aim? Its plausibility depends, in part, on the thesis that what *is* observed is basically what *would* be observed. This is supposedly how we can retain our knowledge of the table's existence and nature, even when not actually observing it. But do we ever *observe* that what is observed is basically what would be observed? It is not clear how we could do so (because, by hypothesis, what only *would* be observed has *not* been observed). Yet if we cannot do so, then phenomenalism relies upon a vital thesis which we could never observe to be true – in which case, phenomenalism goes beyond what we can observe, strictly speaking. Is it therefore not really empiricist, after all? Is this a fundamental restriction upon empiricism's explanatory reach?

Question 10.6 Is being a good person partly a matter of what one *would* do in various circumstances? Does this include circumstances which one will never in fact occupy? If so, is it possible that you will never know that you are a good person – because you never know how you would act in situations you will never enter? Do you know right now how well you *would* act if forced to fight in a war, say? Is such knowledge purely observational?

Perception and reliability

Typically, we assume that there can be observational knowledge of the world, because we take it that *perception* is a source of knowledge: 'I know it's there, because I see it.' One reason for such confidence could be our presuming that in general perception is a *reliable* way of forming some kinds of view (in the sense of reliability introduced in Chapter 8 (Reliabilism)). Specifically, it is likely to give us accurate views regarding many physical aspects of our surroundings.

However, what makes perception reliable (when it is)? A common suggestion is that it is because perception includes an appropriate *causal* link between perceiver and perceived. You see a cat, in part because the cat's being where it is causes an appropriate sensory reaction within you. Because the cat is there, it seems to you that there is a cat there; you thereupon believe that it is there; and, all else being equal, your belief has been formed reliably; that is, it is likely to be true.

But could some causal interactions between objects and your sensory organs fail to be giving you perceptual knowledge? Suppose that, unbeknownst to you, some scientists are manipulating your brain. (An appropriate computer chip was implanted in it last night, as you slept.) They have resolved to give you an idea of a dog whenever a cat is in front of you. On this occasion, they make a mistake – the result being your having the *accurate* idea of a cat walking in front of you. So, there is a causal process, beginning with the cat's entering the room, involving the scientists' bungled intervention, ending with your forming an apparently sensory idea, accurately mirroring the cat's being in front of you. Are you really observing the cat's presence, though? Do you *see* the cat?

Or is there too much luck and accidentality in your gaining that idea, no matter how accurate it is? Is this so weird or deviant a causal chain that you are not really perceiving the cat? Is genuine perception inherently standard or normal? Perhaps even an observation with an unusual content ('No one has ever seen *that* before') requires a stable causal link to the relevant part of reality. Otherwise (you might think), an experience could feel like a real perception without actually being one.

An alternative possible interpretation is that those causal chains, although deviant, are not too much so. Perhaps you do perceive – but luckily – the cat in front of you, even with those scientists manipulating you. They try to prevent your perceiving the cat; have they failed? Recall (from Chapter 9 (Knowing luckily)) the possibility that even within Gettier cases there is knowledge. May we interpret the present case similarly? The knowledge within a Gettier case would be lucky, poor knowledge. Could some observational knowledge be like that, due to perceiving sometimes being like that – lucky, poor? Perhaps an aspect of the world can be observed accurately – yet not so reliably, hence not so well. Might there be both better and worse – although equally accurate – perceptions of some aspect of the world?

Question 10.7 Do people too often observe only what they want to observe? ('You see just that aspect of the situation, because it's all you want to see.') In order to avoid that failing, should we seek to be fully objective? Yet is that so easy? Would your wanting to be fully objective imply your desiring to observe, at least sometimes, not only what you want to observe? And how could you satisfy this overall desire? If you were to do so, would you still be observing, in an overall way, only as you want to observe? ('You *want* to be fully objective. So, you can't *be* fully objective.')

Hume on causation

Hume's discussion of causation is one of empiricism's most substantial contributions to philosophy. What can we observe of causal powers and structures within the world? We talk routinely of forces, actions, influences – objects affecting other objects, one event bringing about another. (Can you imagine a world containing no causality? Try to do so, right now. Did your reading that previous sentence cause you to make that attempt to imagine there being no causality?) But can we know these causal aspects of the world empirically?

It depends on what causation is. Many people would say that it is a strong *connection* between two events, with one's necessitating the other. However, have you ever really observed that kind of link? Hume denied that anyone could do so. His view was that we are restricted to observing, at best, patterns of association, rather than any further links or connections.

Test his claim for yourself. Watch a match being struck and a flame ensuing. Watch another match being struck, with another flame ensuing. We could prolong this pattern at will; we readily call it a causal pattern. But Hume's claim was that no one – and this includes the scientists among us – can observe an underlying necessitation. Observation, no matter how sophisticated, will reveal only one event being followed by another. No matter how many matches are struck, and regardless of how closely they are observed, nothing beyond a regularity is observed. We perceive at most a regular succession – a *constant conjunction* (as Hume called it) between struck match and match aflame. Perhaps continued investigation will uncover a further regularity that helps to explain this one. Even so, we will never observe a further connection underlying – and different in fundamental nature from – such observable regularities.

We could never observe any such connection, because in each instance the two events involved in the causal interaction are *distinct existences* (to use another of Hume's favoured phrases). Neither a match's striking, nor a flame's occurring, literally includes the other. First there is the one; then – even if swiftly – there is the other, metaphysically distinct from the first. Although we might infer that there is a hidden link, this inference goes beyond any direct observational support we could have for it. We cannot observe the link as such; we can observe only the 'before' and the 'after'. To infer that the extra link is present anyway is to go where observation as such cannot take us. So, any claim that a further causal link underlies what is observed is either knowledge which is not purely observational – or it is not knowledge at all. Can there be wholly non-observational knowledge (supported only by pure reason, not observation), or at least knowledge whose support blends observation with reason? Alternatively, might there be no knowledge of the world's workings? The next two chapters, in turn, address these two questions.

Question 10.8   If you were to own a manufacturing company, and if a strong correlation were to be discovered between your company's product and a dangerous illness, would you refuse to accept that this is a causal pattern – until something more than a strong correlation is found? How could that occur, though? Would it be morally irresponsible of you not to treat the strong correlation *as if* it is causal, at any rate? Should you voluntarily cease trading, on moral grounds, until further tests are performed? Do businesses have moral rights to continue trading indefinitely?

Non-inferential knowledge

Philosophers often treat the question of whether we have any purely observational knowledge as being that of whether some observational knowledge is *non-inferential*. (Sometimes, it is called the question of whether any knowledge is *foundational* and observational.) For a piece of knowledge to be non-inferential is for its support to include no reasoning or inference – even unconsciously – from other views. So, purely observational knowledge is non-inferential if it is supported simply by the senses, needing no intellectual 'construction' or organisation or arguable classification, requiring no reasoning supporting or explaining whatever data the senses are providing. Is there any such knowledge? This is an ancient – yet ongoing – philosophical controversy.

Suppose that once more, as you sit there, a cat wanders into the room. 'That looks like a cat,' you might think. And perhaps this belief of yours is purely observational; after all, it talks explicitly of how something appears to you. However, comparatively few of your beliefs are like that. Generally, your speech and thought aim to describe parts of the surrounding world, not only elements in your mental experiences: you want to think 'That is a cat,' not only 'That looks like a cat.' Without beliefs like 'That's a person,' 'That's a man,' 'That's a woman,' and so on, your mind will founder and your life will stumble. Yet won't your support for such views need to be *inferential*? It is hard (if even possible) for you to know 'directly' – purely by sight – that an object in front of you is a cat. Your belief, 'That's a cat,' might well have to be supported by such reasoning (even if unconsciously) as the following:

That looks like a cat, and whatever looks like a cat is a cat. So, that's a cat.

In striving to know about the world, do you rely routinely upon a presumed capacity to *reason* like that (even when unaware of doing so)?

That question has a veiled significance. For what if reason *fails* to be a way to gain knowledge? What if the silentness and hiddenness it often possesses render it uncheckable when being used? Maybe you assume that your views are well supported by your capacity to reason; yet might that be unsupported wishful thinking on your part? Even if your senses are good, *what if your reason is not*? Then you possess dramatically less knowledge than you believe yourself to have. If there is very little non-inferential knowledge, observation on its own provides scant knowledge. So, we must ascertain whether our powers of reason – our intellects – can intervene to give us much, if any, knowledge. We presume that our intellects are dependable accompaniments to our senses. Are we right to trust our powers of reason?

Further reading

On observational knowledge in general:

D.M. Armstrong, *Perception and the Physical World* (New York: The Humanities Press, 1961).

Roderick M. Chisholm, *Theory of Knowledge*, 3rd edn (Englewood Cliffs, NJ: Prentice Hall, 1989), ch. 5.

Jonathan Dancy (ed.), *Perceptual Knowledge* (Oxford: Oxford University Press, 1988).

Richard A. Fumerton, *Metaphysical and Epistemological Problems of Perception* (Lincoln, NB: University of Nebraska Press, 1985).

Robert J. Swartz (ed.), *Perceiving, Sensing, and Knowing* (Garden City, NY: Anchor Books, 1965).

On empiricism's basic idea:
David Hume, *An Enquiry Concerning Human Understanding*, secs I–III.

On representationalism:
J.L. Austin, *Sense and Sensibilia* (Oxford: Clarendon Press, 1962).
Frank Jackson, *Perception: A Representative Theory* (Cambridge: Cambridge University Press, 1977).

For Berkeley's idealism:
George Berkeley, *A Treatise Concerning the Principles of Human Knowledge*.

On phenomenalism:
A.J. Ayer, *The Foundations of Empirical Knowledge* (London: Macmillan, 1979 [1940]).

On perception and reliability:
William P. Alston, *The Reliability of Sense Perception* (Ithaca, NY: Cornell University Press, 1993).

For Hume on causality:
David Hume, *An Enquiry Concerning Human Understanding*, sec. VII.

On non-inferential knowledge:
Laurence BonJour, *The Structure of Empirical Knowledge* (Cambridge, MA: Harvard University Press, 1985), ch. 2.
Roderick M. Chisholm, *The Foundations of Knowing* (Minneapolis, MN: University of Minnesota Press, 1982).

Pure Reason

Rationalism

Chapter 10 ended with these questions:

> Without reason's help, does observation ever give us knowledge? Yet how powerful is reason? Can it ever provide knowledge on its own? Is some knowledge gained *purely* via reason?

Many philosophers have suggested that our unaided intellects do possess the capacity to give us knowledge. Those philosophers are generally called *rationalists*. Whereas empiricists insist that ultimately all knowledge is observational, rationalists claim that at least some knowledge is wholly non-observational. ('But what if all knowledge is a *blend* of observation and reason?' Then neither rationalism nor empiricism is quite right. The section, Kant on *a priori* knowledge, presents a famous attempt to find some such blend. Chapter 12 will discuss whether, even when we use both observation and reason, knowledge is possible.)

Rationalists agree with empiricists that people can have knowledge by being rational – using reason. But rationalists, unlike empiricists, think that some knowledge is *purely* rational. That is, rationalists say that some views are well supported in a way that is wholly intellectual or reasoned, or that comes from a non-observational kind of insight. In order to make a view knowledge in this way, intellect suffices; senses are not needed.

Of course, because you have various sensory capacities, you might believe that your observations contribute to all of your knowledge. However, even if in fact they do so, does it remain *possible* for you to have some wholly non-observational knowledge? Imagine losing your sensory powers. Would you thereby lose your ability to reason? You could not gain new empirical knowledge of the world. Might you gain new knowledge anyway?

Question 11.1   Does being a person require you to be able, at times, to think wholly abstractly? Does it involve a capacity to think perfectly rationally? (Do you often think like that? For how many minutes at a time can you do so?) Do only people think in such ways? How could we know that no other animals do so? (Should we treat them differently if we decide that they think more, rather than less, like us?) What is it about us that enables us to think at all? If it is our ability to perceive the world, is none of our thinking *pure* reasoning? Are we more fundamentally observers than reasoners?

A *priori* knowledge

Philosophers have long called wholly non-observational knowledge *a priori* knowledge. It is knowledge which is supported non-observationally, presumably via pure reason. It is supported even *prior* to any observations contributing to its support. And it is traditionally contrasted with *a posteriori* knowledge, whose support component is at least partly observational. A view is *a posteriori* knowledge only *after* enough pertinent observations become part of its support.

What might be some examples of *a priori* knowledge? Historically, rationalists have cited three main kinds:

Mathematical, such as: $7 + 5 = 12$.
Logical, such as: If A implies B, and if B implies C, then A implies C.
Metaphysical, such as: No physical object could be red and green all over at once.

These are comparatively everyday cases. But already subtle questions arise.

Necessity   Each of those examples seems to be not only true but necessarily so. Philosophers generally distinguish *necessary* truths from *contingent* ones: any truth is necessary or contingent, not both. A necessary truth could not have been false: supposedly, there is no possible way for $7 + 5$ not to equal 12. But a contingent truth, although in fact true, might have been false: you exist, yet you might not have done so. Contingent truths reflect how reality happens – without having had – to be. Are contingent truths known only by observation? Is part of pure reason's appeal its capacity to give us what observation cannot – namely, knowledge of necessities, knowledge of what could not have failed to be as it is? Traditionally, rationalists thought so. They claimed that, purely via rational insight, we can know objects' *essences* (as explained in Chapter 6 (Essentialism)).

Facts   Can there be substantial *a priori* knowledge – *a priori* knowledge of genuine facts in the world? Many thinkers have claimed to possess some such knowledge. If there is a God, for example, is this knowable just by thinking hard about it? And what about our meta-physical understanding of ourselves? Might you know *a priori* what a person is – without testing your concept of a person on observations of people? Can you know *a priori* – simply by pure thought – that people are inherently important beings? Such questions could continue indefinitely. (Indeed, some philosophers have thought that philosophy itself is an *a priori* way of thinking. Can you know the answers to this book's questions without observing the world?) In this chapter, I concentrate on mathematical knowledge. Is it possible for you to know *a priori* that $7 + 5 = 12$? Would this be knowledge of a substantial fact, one helping to constitute the world?

Question 11.2   If children know less of the world than adults do, might they have a correlatively purer reason – more welcoming of odd yet imaginable possibilities, more capable of rational insights? Or do children not even have real reason? Are they as restricted rationally as they are experientially? If so, might they overcome these restrictions as they mature? How long would that take? Does it occur automatically? Or is a capacity for reason only acquired with effort? Might it require a skill which not everyone has? If everyone acquires it automatically, is it trivial, not worth having? Even once it is present, could it be lost – perhaps through age or disuse?

Plato's rationalism

Probably the first great rationalist was Plato. He is associated with a few rationalist patterns of thought. Here are two that he seems to have advanced.

Knowledge versus belief   In his dialogue *Republic*, Plato advocated an extremely strict rationalism. When you know, he claimed, what you know are eternal truths – necessary truths. (This includes knowing the eternally and necessarily existing Forms.) What you do not know is the observable world. Although you can have beliefs about the world around you, these are not knowledge. This is not simply because knowing is more demanding than believing. In the *Republic*, Plato thought that knowledge and belief are metaphysically disjoint: you cannot both believe and know the one truth. (People often say 'I don't believe it; I know it.') Belief is what perception gives you, as your senses respond to the changeable world. Knowledge is what reason gives you, as *it* responds to the *un*changeable world. You can know – by pure reason – that $7 + 5 = 12$. You will only believe – by observation – that there is a frog on your shoulder. (You're too late. It's gone now.) Perhaps you can know – by pure reason – what the Form of the Good (that is, what goodness itself) is like. But although you can believe – by observation – that a particular person is good, you never know that he or she is good.

Knowledge as perception?   In a later dialogue, the *Theaetetus*, Plato argued against the thesis that knowledge is perception (a thesis famously advocated at that time by Theaetetus). Plato's arguments against this empiricist thesis involved some themes we have already met.

First, he dismissed that thesis because (it seems) he regarded it as *relativist*. (We discussed relativism in Chapter 8 (Epistemic relativism).) He argued as follows. A perception as such is only an individual experience. It is fleeting, transitory. But knowledge is *infallibly* of what is true. So, if knowledge were perception, it would be an infallible experience of what is true. However, perceptions differ routinely, from person to person, moment to moment. Hence, they could infallibly reveal only a world that is *itself* changing routinely, in harmony with how the perceptions themselves do. That would be a world in constant transition, a world without stability. Yet (thought Plato) we really cannot understand how the world could be like that. Our terms would cease applying to it; our thoughts would fall apart. There would be no continuing you to be referred to as 'you'; there would be no persisting frog to be called 'frog'; and so on. There would be only 'this-now' and 'that-now'. Knowledge, therefore, must be something other than mere observation. It cannot be answerable only to how an individual seems to view the world. It cannot be that insubstantial.

So (inferred Plato), knowledge involves reason. This is his version of Chapter 10's (Non-inferential knowledge) argument for little, if any, observational knowledge being non-inferential. In effect, he says that all apparently observational knowledge is inferential – reasoned. You do not know observationally that the object in front of you is a person; there is knowledge only insofar as you judge or infer or interpret that the object is a person. Your perceptions as such are merely experiences that any animal could have! Real knowledge requires a 'higher' kind of reason; there is no purely observational knowledge.

Question 11.3   Could a person already possess some knowledge when born? That is, might there be people with *innate* knowledge? Would everyone have some? Is it part of the *essence* of a person to be born with some rational insights? How much such insight might there be? What would it be about? And what will make it knowledge – rather than merely instinctive thinking? Are instinctive views less likely than reflective, considered, views to be true? Or are instinctive views knowledge *because* they are instinctive?

Descartes's rationalist method

One of the greatest modern rationalists was Descartes. We have already (in Chapter 1 (Descartes on what persons are)) seen his rationalism generating part of his metaphysical theory of what it is to be a person. A few more words on his underlying epistemology are needed, though, because it has been crucial to philosophy's subsequent development. At its heart (as that section indicated) was a *method of doubt*. In Chapter 12 (Descartes's dreaming argument, Descartes's evil genius), we will consider Descartes's most notorious specific doubts. In this section, I outline only his general rationalist strategy.

Like Plato, Descartes assumed that all knowledge is infallible: a view needs to receive infallibilist support if it is to be knowledge. Also like Plato, Descartes thought that some significant views are indeed known infallibly – and not via observation. His *Cogito* was one such view; it was not the only one. There are some crucial truths that the *natural light of reason* (as Descartes termed it) illuminates for us, and upon which all knowledge ultimately depends. Think about your everyday views, those you regard as knowledge. How do they arise? Often we venerate culture and upbringing as a source of views. ('That's where I obtain my way of viewing the world.') But should we do so, insofar as we care about infallibly seeking truth? To Descartes, one's worldly background (like so much else) could easily lead one to accept what is false. Cultural approval is not infallible. It can even be a *poor* guide to what is true (as Chapter 8 (Epistemic relativism) remarked). Are we able to improve on uncritically accepting what has seemed true so far in our lives?

Descartes would have asked you this:

> Could you cast off all your present opinions, even those of which you are confident? Do you have the ability to begin again as a knowledge-seeker – more carefully this time? Can you contemplate open-mindedly every possible source of falsity in your thinking?

Descartes apparently set himself this goal. His quest was modelled upon mathematical inquiry. That was where truth was most clearly to be found. There lay infallibility. And can we extend such thinking to knowledge in general? Is disciplined and rigorous reason the way to gain knowledge? Descartes thought so. Even if we concentrate, we will make mistakes – unless we first find some views which cannot rationally be doubted. Find these; use them as bases for the most secure reasoning possible; knowledge will ensue, based wholly on reason. And to vary this method is to run risks that chase away knowledge.

It is instructive to compare that rationalist method of Descartes's with Popper's empiricist one (in Chapter 8 (Popper and testability)). Popper urged us to try *falsifying* our views. This is definitive of scientific inquiry, he believed. But he used that idea more cautiously than

Descartes employed the idea of knowledge as ultimately being based on doubt. A view which is not yet falsified, according to Popper, is corroborated only thus far. He was reluctant to infer that it is knowledge. After all, the world might falsify it tomorrow! (All swans, it was believed in the world of science, were white – and then Australian black swans came to science's attention.) Descartes relentlessly sought doubt, including falsification. However, he thought that if reason has been unable to doubt a view, then the view must be true: his *Cogito* resulted from this process of thought. If your reason has been unable to doubt your existence as a thinking thing, for instance, then – according to Descartes – your reason should infer that you are a thinking thing: you know, via reason, that you think and thereby exist. If your reason has been unable to doubt that there is a God, say, then your reason tells you that there is a God; Descartes's reason told *him* this. In principle, therefore, reason can uncover some of the world's metaphysical facts.

But are our minds really so powerful? Popper accepted that the observable world can surprise us, mocking our previous efforts at understanding it through our senses. Is pure reason also vulnerable to being surprised, even overthrown? Could it nonetheless give us knowledge? We return to these questions in the section, Fallible *a priori* knowledge.

Question 11.4   Could an imperfect world contain perfect knowledge? If you do everything else in ways that could be improved (and don't you?), can you reasonably expect to be so good a thinker as to gain much infallible knowledge? Is it reasonable of you to anticipate gaining even *some* infallible knowledge? How imperfect a being are you? (And how do you know the answer to that question? Do you know perfectly that you are imperfect?)

Kant on *a priori* knowledge

Probably the most powerful investigation of rationalism's prospects was by the German philosopher Immanuel Kant (1724–1804), particularly in his grand *Critique of Pure Reason*. I will mention a few of his ideas.

A priori *spatial, temporal, and categorial knowledge*   How do we know of the world around us? In general (argued Kant), we do so through experience. But experience is surprisingly complicated. It involves more than sensations, because these have to be guided. We must interpret whatever 'raw data' the world throws at our sense-organs; only then are we having real experiences. So, we have a prior ability to interpret the sensations. We already have in mind what Kant called *forms* of sensing ('sensibility') and *categories* of thought – fundamental frameworks and concepts within us, with which we turn sensations into experiences. We know, prior to having sensations, that they will be of a *spatial* and *temporal* world with a geometrical and mathematical form. And we know, prior to having experiences, that we will experience the world as containing *substances*, which interact *causally*, and so on. (Hume was mistaken, in Kant's view, when seeking *all* knowledge of causality through observation: we have some of it – the initial knowledge that it is causation we will experience – prior to perceiving specific causal interactions.) Knowledge as basic as that categorial knowledge, or as that knowledge of space and time, is not supported *by* perceptions. Instead, it is applied *to* perceptions – thereby helping to create full experiences as such. In this way, you have some *a priori* knowledge with which you approach the world – and without which you could not experience that world. These are basic ways in which a mind cannot avoid interpreting the world.

Yet do we thereby know the world? Or are we perhaps knowing *a priori* only how, in general ways, the world is bound to *appear* to us? And is there a possibility of our minds being bound to interpret sensations in ways that are *misleading* as to what the world is like? Kant distinguished between objects as they appear to us and objects as they are in themselves. (He called these, respectively, *phenomena* and *noumena*.) And only the former, he held, could be known by us. Like other perceiving creatures, we cannot know what the world is like in itself. After all, any knowledge of the world relies on our senses interacting with the world, hence on its somehow appearing to us. We do not know the world by way of a detached and purely reasoned perspective on the world itself – on what it is like without appearing to us. We cannot even form specific and informative conceptions of what the world is like, beyond how it might appear to us.

Any such conception would be *a priori* knowledge (if knowledge at all). So, there are limits on what we can know *a priori*. We cannot know eternal metaphysical truths beyond what is observable. We have neither Platonic knowledge of Forms, nor those metaphysical insights that Descartes thought were revealed by reason (such as knowledge of an unobservable God). In Kant's view, although we can believe that there is a God, we cannot know that there is one. Pure reason strives for such knowledge – but is doomed to fail.

Synthetic a priori knowledge   Could reason nonetheless give us *a priori* knowledge of mathematics, for example? Kant thought so. And he sought to explain why this would be informative knowledge. He introduced the idea of synthetic *a priori* knowledge. Mathematical knowledge was like this, he argued (as were spatial, temporal, and categorial *a priori* knowledge). The distinction between *analytic* truths and *synthetic* ones was Kant's. In an analytic truth, he said, a concept is analysed, with some of its components thereby being made explicit – as in, for instance, 'All bachelors are unmarried.' (Part of the meaning of the term 'bachelor' is conveyed by 'being unmarried'.) An analytic truth is thus 'inward looking', somewhat trivial. It is true merely because of how the meanings of its terms relate to each other. It therefore tells us nothing about the wider world – such as whether there are any bachelors. A synthetic truth, on the other hand, brings together – it synthesises – some more or less independent concepts. Empirical truths, such as that bachelors exist, are synthetic. But, intriguingly, so are mathematical ones, claimed Kant. For example, the term '7 + 5 =' means only 7's *being added to 5 to give whatever result it gives*; and this does not *include* what '12' means. Strictly, the result of any particular process of addition awaits discovery. Kant thought that synthetic truths contain real information, whereas analytic truths do not.

Mathematical truths would remain necessary: 7 + 5 cannot help but equal 12. Yet they would not be trivial. There is genuine information in them. Did Kant thus help us to understand how there can be substantial *a priori* knowledge of at least some of the world's eternal aspects?

Question 11.5 'There cannot be knowledge of *kinds* of action being morally right or being morally wrong, because situations vary so much. That complexity prevents our accurately generalising.' (But isn't that a generalisation itself about moral truth?) Could there be *a priori* knowledge of some general moral truths? For instance, do you know – just by thinking – that it is morally wrong to use other people as means rather than valuing them as ends in themselves? How *much* thinking would be required in order to have that knowledge *a priori*? (Could you have it only as part of a larger moral system?) Are observations also needed to support that piece of knowledge? How can you *observe* something's being an end in itself? Is this a real property possessed by each person? Or is it merely a concept we might – or might not – choose to apply to people?

Mill's radical empiricism

In spite of Kant's generally acknowledged genius, not all later philosophers have accepted his theories. (In philosophy, respect is not always manifested in agreement.) Might he have been mistaken about there even being *a priori* knowledge? The prominent empiricist John Stuart Mill thought that there is none. His fame is due mainly to his writings in ethical theory (helping to develop utilitarianism) and political philosophy (defending the importance of liberty). But he also argued vigorously that no one has *a priori* knowledge.

How do you know that 7 + 5 = 12? You know it *observationally*, claimed Mill. You know it by generalising (even if unconsciously) from observations of the world. You do not observe abstract numbers as such. You observe combinations and additions of actual objects. The truth that $7 + 5 = 12$ might seem to be abstract and non-observational. However, this is because a purely numerical view is about everything equally. Accordingly, in principle it receives constant observational support from everything. But in principle, this implies, the world could also *falsify* it tomorrow. Because that has not yet happened, we have become accustomed to accepting the view that $7 + 5 = 12$ is true – indeed, necessarily true. We have relaxed; we have not remained vigilant, open to the possibility of finding that $7 + 5 \neq 12$. Our belief that $7 + 5 = 12$ is simply much *better* supported than whatever views we are actively testing; that mathematical belief is not supported in some quite different *way*.

Philosophers usually find Mill's radical empiricism unconvincing. He would not be perturbed by this. Consider how he responded to the following sort of objection:

> There is a deep difference between, say, the world containing no kangaroos, and $7 + 5$ not equalling 12. I can conceive of the former; I cannot conceive of the latter. Hence, mathematical truths must be true.

This was the heart of Mill's response:

> Is your inability to conceive of something a perfect indicator of its being impossible? Surely not. Maybe the reason why you cannot conceive of it is that you have become comfortable with your current ways of thinking. Inflexibility of thought has triumphed – without your realising it. What you interpret as insightfulness into what is necessary could well be, instead, your inability to recognise and transcend a conceptual limitation of yours. (And the onus is on you, if you credit yourself with possessing an extra and distinctive mental power, to show why you are not mistaking a mental limitation for a further mental ability.)

Mill was not saying that he knew with certainty that no one has *a priori* insight into such truths as that $7 + 5 = 12$. But he was saying that empiricism provides a simpler – *yet good enough* – explanation of data (such as people being unable to conceive of some particular view's being false) which we might think reveal our possessing *a priori* insight into what must be true. We should not rush to think of ourselves – somewhat arrogantly? – as having intellectual powers which we are not rationally *obliged* to regard ourselves as having.

Question 11.6   Could pure thought ever be rationally counter-productive? Might it hinder one's observing what is happening around one? Is it more likely than observation to lead to one's adopting an ideology? What *is* an ideology? Are all ideologies too far removed from observational checks and balances to be knowledge? (Are religions ideologies? Can political views become ideologies? What of economic theories?) Do some or all ideologies involve too much thinking or feeling, too little observing?

Logical empiricism

Not all empiricists have been as dismissive as Mill of the concept of *a priori* knowledge. Notably, the *logical empiricists* (also called logical positivists or, more simply, positivists) were not.

For around half of the twentieth century, logical empiricism was highly influential. Centred upon Vienna, especially in the 1920s and 1930s, it attracted eminent scientists, mathematicians, and philosophers. They combined empiricism with formal logic, seeking a scientific philosophy of thought's and language's many manifestations. Probably their core concept was that of empirical verifiability. They argued that any view for which there are no possible *supportive observations* says nothing – literally nothing. 'But no view could be like that,' you might say. 'On the contrary,' claimed the positivists, 'ethics and religion and metaphysics have this flaw.' (What is it for an observation to support a view, though? It is this positivist conception of empirical support which Popper was refining, when developing his idea of empirical falsifiability: Chapter 8 (Popper and testability).) For instance, your views on what is ethically wrong are expressive, not descriptive. They express emotional attitudes – nothing more – and so they cannot be observationally supported as being true.

Nonetheless, logical empiricists did accept that there could be *a priori* knowledge. How is this possible? Isn't *a priori* knowledge always knowledge of what is *not* observational? The positivists' answer was blunt: *A priori* knowledge is not knowledge of *facts*. In knowing that $7 + 5 = 12$ (they would have said), you are simply understanding meanings. In this way, logical empiricists generalised the Kantian idea of an analytic truth. To them (and theirs became the dominant empiricist view on this topic), all mathematical truths are analytic – true merely by meaning.

This meant (said the positivists) that mathematical truths are just *conventional* truths – reflecting only the existence of various linguistic conventions about meaning, about how to use mathematical terms. 'Once we know the meanings of the terms being used, we know that $7 + 5 = 12$. We do not thereby know some further aspect of reality.' But this positivist claim is easy to make, hard to understand. Here are two possible interpretations of it.

Actual uses   Were positivists saying that, in knowing that $7 + 5 = 12$, you know, via observation, merely how people actually use the terms '7', '+', '5', and so on? This would make mathematical knowledge observational, not *a priori* (and so we would be reaching for a version of Mill's radical empiricism). Most philosophers resist this interpretation because it seems to make mathematical truths too weak. Will $7 + 5$ really no longer equal 12 if, for example, most people begin denying that it does?

Correct uses   Should we therefore regard conventionalism as saying that *a priori* knowledge is knowledge of how words *should* be used? You are asked 'What does $7 + 5$ equal?' You should answer '12'. But what is the source of this 'should'? Is '12' the answer you should give, simply because other people think so? That would return us to the first interpretation. If you wish to avoid that analysis, should you say that '12' is the correct answer because it is *true*? Presumably so. Then what makes it true? In knowing that $7 + 5 = 12$, you know some fact; which one? (And *where* in the world is it?) If your knowledge that $7 + 5 = 12$ is knowledge of something that would not exist if we had never adopted various conventions for using mathematical terms, is it knowledge only of a socially constructed truth (Chapter 7 (Social constructivism))? (Couldn't we have chosen different linguistic conventions for using mathematical terms?) And would this make mathematical knowledge rather trivial – knowledge only of rules governing an arbitrary way of speaking and thinking? If conventionalism is accepted, must we accept that even pure reason never reveals a world of mathematical facts existing in themselves? Do we lack good support for believing that such facts exist?

Question 11.7   Why do you ever think poorly? Presumably, you do not realise at the time that you are doing so; why not? What, if anything, obscures your recognising this failing at the time? (Do you simply not *want* to notice it?) Even afterwards, when thinking that your earlier thinking was poor, might you still be thinking poorly? Or might you only now be thinking poorly (not having been doing so earlier)? What does all of this imply about your powers of reason? Are they poorer than you know? (Yet how well can you know this?)

Fallible *a priori* knowledge

How limited are our intellects? Are there boundaries beyond which they falter, then fall? You ask yourself, 'What is 56×75?' You answer, with some hesitation, '4200 ... or is it 4300? ... no, it's 4200.' Not being perfectly confident, you repeat your reasoning. Perhaps that is appropriate; you are a fallible mathematical reasoner. Your answer is correct, though, as your calculations generally are. You are reliable at reaching true mathematical beliefs like this one. Is your belief therefore not only true but well supported?

If so, is it possible to have fallible knowledge which is also *a priori*? You reasoned; you did not observe. You did it well enough to reach – with some reliability – the correct conclusion. Accordingly, unless we require *a priori* knowledge to be infallible, we may infer that you have some knowledge which is both *a priori* and fallible. We would be accepting that pure reason can be fallible even when providing us with knowledge: *a priori* knowledge could be fallible. Pure reason would be a distinctive *way* of gaining knowledge – without setting a special *standard* of knowledge.

This possibility is important, because over the centuries so many people have been tempted by the idea of our having a faculty of pure reason that is infallible. They have regarded pure reason as a sort of *perfectly and inevitably accurate* rationality, undistracted by the passing perceptual show. But why must pure reason be like that? Reason is pure when not at all observational; this does not guarantee its perfection in any sense other than that of being 'perfectly non-observational'. You often perceive inaccurately and incompletely; why would you always reason accurately or completely? You do not always notice every aspect of a situation when observing it; don't you often overlook mistakes in your reasoning, too? Even when thinking about a narrow topic, might there be pertinent possibilities which you fail to take into account?

It is hard to reason well. It might be impossible to reason infallibly. For example, if you are to have infallible knowledge of what you think on some topic, must you check all of your views? ('Which of my views are relevant to this topic? Do any of them clash with each other? Are my views as a whole on this topic coherent?') Yet perhaps you cannot do that. Maybe there are too many views to check. Might some be hidden? And even if you could be aware of the entirety, properly comparing each with each is far from easy. For a start, how full is your grasp of logic? How fine-tuned is your understanding of the meanings, the many implications, of each of your beliefs? And what of those beliefs you lack but *should* have (given what else you believe)? No one is perfect in all these possible – and potentially endless – respects. So, if *a priori* knowledge needs to be infallible, quite possibly no one ever has any *a priori* knowledge.

In which case, we return to where this section began – asking whether pure reason can give us at least *fallible a priori* knowledge. That question leads to these ones. Can you have *good-though-not-perfect* non-observational knowledge that 7 + 5 = 12? (Would it be a well, although fallibly, supported true belief that $7 + 5 = 12$?) Could you improve that knowledge (probably by improving your reasoned support for it)? This might be hard; yet is it possible? And is this part of the point of thinking well and abstractly – first gaining, then improving, what one hopes is *a priori* knowledge (even while accepting that such knowledge will never be infallible)? If we do have any *a priori* knowledge, we should suspect that it is fallible at best. But isn't this possibility still more optimistic than not?

Further reading

On rationalism and *a priori* knowledge in general:

Laurence BonJour, *In Defense of Pure Reason* (Cambridge: Cambridge University Press, 1998).

Roderick M. Chisholm, *Theory of Knowledge*, 3rd edn (Englewood Cliffs, NJ: Prentice Hall, 1989), ch. 4.

Philip Hanson and Bruce Hunter (eds), *Return of the A Priori* (Calgary: University of Calgary Press, 1992).

Saul A. Kripke, *Naming and Necessity* (Cambridge, MA: Harvard University Press, 1980).

Paul K. Moser (ed.), *A Priori Knowledge* (New York: Oxford University Press, 1987).

For Plato's rationalism about knowledge:

Plato, *Republic* 475b–480, and *Theaetetus* 151d–186e.

For Descartes's rationalist method:

René Descartes, *Discourse on Method*, Parts II, IV.

For Kant on *a priori* knowledge:

Immanuel Kant, *Critique of Pure Reason*, trans. Norman Kemp Smith. (A more accessible work is Kant's *Prolegomena to any Future Metaphysics*.)

For Mill on *a priori* knowledge:

John Stuart Mill, *A System of Logic*, Book II, chs IV–VI.

On logical empiricism:

A.J. Ayer, *Language, Truth and Logic*, 2nd edn (Harmondsworth: Penguin, 1946 [1936]).

A.J. Ayer (ed.), *Logical Positivism* (Glencoe, IL: The Free Press, 1959).

On fallibility and *a priori* knowledge:

Christopher Cherniak, *Minimal Rationality* (Cambridge, MA: The MIT Press, 1986).

Alvin I. Goldman, *Pathways to Knowledge* (New York: Oxford University Press, 2002), ch. 2.

Sceptical Doubts

Blended knowledge?

What knowledge can your senses as such give you? What knowledge can reason as such provide? Chapters 10 and 11 posed those questions. But surely (you might wonder) focussing on them was unlikely to illuminate much, if any, knowledge. Don't we generally – even always – gain knowledge by *blending* those two cognitive capacities? Must we sense *and* think if we are to gain much knowledge? Are both sensing and thinking necessary if we are to gain even some knowledge?

Kant thought so. Reason and observation must unite, he claimed (in his *Critique of Pure Reason*), if a person is to have knowledge. Thinking without sensing is empty. Sensing without thinking is blind. Again, each of thinking and sensing is needed.

Yet is a blend of thinking and sensing ever *sufficient* for knowing? Even when reason and observation are combined, might problems persist for our gaining knowledge? We tend to be confident that if we pay attention to our surroundings and if we think carefully, we accumulate a great deal of knowledge. Could that optimism be misguided? Might we actually be surprisingly poor at knowing reality? That possibility is what this chapter discusses. We will consider some ways in which – or so various philosophers have thought – our powers of observation and of reason, even when blended, fall short of supplying good support for our views. Each of reason and observation on its own has limitations. Can we be sure that combining them overcomes those limitations? Might observation and reason never fully harmonise? Maybe combining them brings its own dangers. Could doing so give us a 'muddied' mind – insufficiently observational, insufficiently reflective? Might observation and reason 'get in each other's way' (instead of helpfully complementing each other)? We will investigate such possibilities.

Question 12.1   Should our minds strive relentlessly not to be mistaken? Or could this sometimes make us too intellectually cautious, more likely to overlook important truths? Are there intellectual dangers, though, in not being cautious enough, in believing on insufficient evidence? Are confident people most likely to be correct? Are they usually the best sources of knowledge? Is feeling confident a good sign of having knowledge? Or does confidence ever mislead people into thinking that they have knowledge? Can people be unwarrantedly confident? (Pol Pot, at his life's end, assured us that his conscience was clear. But *should* it have been clear? Was the clarity of his conscience inadequate evidence of his not having been responsible for much evil?)

Scepticisms

One of philosophy's perennial preoccupations has been the question of whether people have the knowledge they think they have. Philosophical *sceptics* have given us much memorable reasoning, arguing for what will strike most of us as being rather remarkable doubts as to our capacity to have much, if any, knowledge.

Historically, scepticism has taken several forms. For example, you could argue, quite radically, that we have no knowledge at all. Then again, you might deny us just one or more specific kinds of knowledge. You might argue for there being no knowledge of moral truths, say, or for there being no knowledge of what the physical world is like. In theory, for any proposed area of human thought, sceptical doubts are possible.

They generally emerge as philosophers ask whether we ever – not merely today or tomorrow, but ever – have sufficiently good *support* for our views. How would you reason sceptically against there being moral knowledge, for instance? The usual approach is to argue that we never have (objectively) good support for our views on what is, or is not, moral – and that we therefore lack moral knowledge. So (this sceptic would claim), regardless of whether it is true that racism is immoral, no one can have objectively good support for believing that it is true – and hence no one can know that racism is immoral. In the sections, Descartes's dreaming argument through to Being freely rational, we meet some sceptical arguments, each of which doubts our ability to have good support for many of our everyday views. Sceptics are nothing if not audacious! (Still, although sceptical arguments differ in details, they reason in similar ways. This will allow us, in the sections, Moore and commonsense through to Improved knowledge, to appreciate some general anti-sceptical ideas.)

Question 12.2   'People should not be judgemental. That is a bad way to be.' But isn't that a judgement about how people should speak and think? 'I don't like to generalise.' Why not? Are generalisations never true? Can't they ever be well sup-ported (even if not infallibly so)? 'We should always be guarded in what we think.' Why? Are all strongly held opinions false or unsupported? Isn't it possible to accept something as true – and then rationally to reject it as false, if the evidence no longer supports it? Or is no change of belief ever rational? Should you be forever loyal to what you already believe? ('Once I believe something to be true, I reject whatever looks like evidence against it.') Or is that merely dogmatic? Is doubt good in itself? Is having an opinion good in itself? When is it right to have no opinion?

Descartes's dreaming argument

Two of the most audacious of all sceptical doubts were Descartes's (as he began applying his method of doubt, described in Chapter 11 (Descartes's rationalist method)). He used these not to accept their sceptical conclusions, but to prepare the way for what he believed to be an understanding of how we have knowledge. (In seeing why sceptical doubts do not deprive us of knowledge, he thought, he would under-stand knowledge better by ascertaining which of its properties render it impervious to these scepticisms.) In this section and the next, respect-ively, I outline these two notorious doubts.

The first is usually known as the dreaming argument. Here is its basic idea:

> Dreams can be life-like, powerful, sustained. When experiencing one like that, you feel as though you are wholly awake, observing the world, living in it. How do you know that you are not dreaming in that way right now? You feel awake. But this is exactly how you would feel if you *were* dreaming in that vivid and 'life-like' manner. And if you do not know that you are not dreaming, then your feeling as if you are observing the world is not your *knowing* the world. Yet such apparently observational experience is the only possible way of gaining knowledge of the world. You therefore gain none!

Do your powers of reason allow you to evade that challenge to the powers of your senses? Far from it (argues this sceptic): even when you feel confident that you are seeing a dog, say, your reason as such should realise that possibly you are dreaming – and that if you were dreaming, you would not realise that you were doing so. You would be dreaming in a 'hidden' way, mistakenly feeling as if you are sensing the world.

This sceptic is not saying that none of your beliefs about the world around you are true. He or she is denying, however, that you can ever know which, if any, of them are true: what seems to be good observa-tional evidence could actually be providing quite poor, if any, support for your beliefs or claims about the world – by being part of a dream. Supposedly, *external world* scepticism is thus established. It denies that one has any knowledge of what the world is like outside one's mind or consciousness. Within your mind dwell appearances or representations, seemingly of a world beyond. You assume that these give you knowledge of that world. But is your assumption incorrect? The external world sceptic thinks so.

Question 12.3 'I'm alive. And racism is immoral.' Are you more confident of the truth of one of those two claims than you are of the other's being true? Do you have equally good evidence for the truth of each claim? If not, then is at least one of those bodies of evidence not as good as it could be? Does this imply that at least one of your two claims is not knowledge? Which is less likely to be knowledge? What would it be, if not knowledge?

Descartes's evil genius

Descartes's sceptical questioning did not end there. He also fashioned a way of doubting all views, not only those about the physical world. Here is the idea behind what has come to be termed Descartes's evil genius (or evil demon) argument:

We do not control the entire world. Perhaps, instead, we are controlled by aspects of it, in powerful and hidden ways. At any rate, might our *thoughts* be what they are due to forces of which we are unaware? Might we even be routinely caused – without realising it – to have false thoughts? Self-deceptive impulses could operate inescapably within us. Or maybe (and this was the possibility described by Descartes) an evil spirit or genius or demon – not God, but something evil with comparable powers – oversees our minds. We rarely, if ever, feel that this is happening. But an evil genius (of the kind described by Descartes) would *make* us feel that we are not being radically deceived. We would seem, to ourselves, to be reasonably accurate observers and thinkers; we would thereby be deceived – as part of the evil genius's malevolent plan!

Even combining sensing with reasoning cannot escape that problem, says this sceptic. Your reason as such should realise that, in spite of everything seeming normal to you right now, there is a possibility of an evil genius deceiving you. (The evil genius could even be allowing you to have that thought!) There are many possible causes of your having had the apparent observations and thoughts you have had during your life – an evil genius being one of those possible causes. No doubt, you think that an evil genius is an *unlikely* cause. But how well supported is that comforting thought? Its seeming unlikely to you that you are being 'toyed with' by an evil genius could *itself* be due to your being 'toyed with' like that. Any thought that has ever appeared in your mind could have been placed there by an evil genius.

Hence, concludes this sceptical reasoning, you know nothing. You even lack knowledge that $7 + 5 = 12$. Nor do you know that there is a physical world around you. You fail to know how you came to exist in this world. For – unfortunately – you do not know that no evil genius is sustaining your existence.

Question 12.4 Are there people whose job it is to disseminate data – but not always knowledge? (Think of public relations 'consultants', for a start.) Often, such people are central to the circulation, within a community, of what we assume is information about governments, individual politicians, companies, entertainers, and so on. Accordingly, how much knowledge do you gain about these organisations and people? In an 'information era', can knowledge become *harder* to obtain – without our always being aware of this? Are we ever being deliberately misled – manipulated – in apparently informative contexts? When 'image' becomes so widely revered, are knowledge and truth being undervalued? Could this harm a society?

Hume on induction

Like Descartes, part of Hume's philosophical fame is due to some sceptical doubts which he developed. His best-known one generated what is called *inductive* scepticism. It doubts our ability to have observationally well supported views about what we have not observed. It thus doubts that inductive thinking provides well supported views. (Induction is one's reasoning, even if unconsciously, from 'the observed to the unobserved', not – as students are often told – from 'the particular to the general'.)

For example, do you have good evidence supporting your belief that the sun will rise tomorrow? And what of your belief that dinosaurs existed millions of years ago? If you have good support for the truth of these beliefs, it is observational (such as evidence of past sunrises, or of dinosaur fossils); you cannot simply call on pure reason to provide genuine support for them. Any good observational support for them would also be inductive, because in each case your observations are supporting a view about something which you have not observed. Nonetheless, let's see how inductive sceptics argue that your belief that the sun will rise tomorrow is not well supported – not even by your past experiences.

Here is the basic idea behind Hume's reasoning:

Each day of your life has begun with a sunrise; you might have observed many of them. Do those experiences support your thinking that if you awake early tomorrow, you will observe another sunrise? No. The world might be about to change in this respect. Although your past observations do not suggest that this will occur, your powers of reason can conceive of its happening. You can imagine many possible ways a world could be; the world's continuing to be as it has been until now (with each new day including a sunrise) is just one of those possible ways it might be after today.

Moreover, according to this inductive sceptic, that shortcoming afflicts even the more cautious belief that a sunrise tomorrow is *likely*. Just as there is a possibility of the sun not rising tomorrow and of the world thereby changing, there is a possibility of the change being so dramatic that nevermore is a sunrise even likely. Right now, you do not believe that such a change is about to occur. But in having that reaction, you are still relying upon evidence of what has occurred in the past: until now, predicting either roughly or exactly in accord with past observations has generally led to accurate views. In other words, inductive thinking has so far been reliable (in Chapter 8's (Reliabilism) sense). Again, though, the past reliability of inductive thinking might be about to be replaced by such thinking's being unreliable. Its past reliability does not prove that it will continue being reliable. You therefore cannot know that such a radical change – from induction's being reliable, to its being unreliable – is even unlikely. Are none of your predictions (even when weakened by 'likely' or 'probably') well supported by your observations? Indeed so, concludes this sceptic. They are not well supported by pure reason alone or by observation alone, or by any blend of pure reason and observation.

Hume did not think that people, after hearing his sceptical reasoning, would cease thinking inductively. (Nor was he perturbed by this.) You will continue believing that the sun (either definitely or probably) will rise tomorrow. Kant regarded the tendency to expect the world to behave causally as an essential and innate aspect of our minds; Hume remarked on people's entrenched *habits* of having such expectations. Can you lose such habits? Can you stop expecting the future to be at least reasonably like the past in relevant respects – even if you cannot really support that expectation? Not according to Hume: We are fundamentally creatures of habit, even when thinking. Hume called this a *sceptical solution* to his sceptical argument. He was saying that even though we cannot have good support (via observation or reason) for beliefs about yet-to-be-observed aspects of the world, we cannot avoid forming such beliefs. Do our human natures thus limit us, leaving us cognitively trapped? (We return to this question in the section, Being freely rational.)

Question 12.5 If it is impossible to have good evidence of what is yet to occur, is it intellectually pointless to plan for good outcomes rather than bad ones? Are we doomed to repeat past mistakes if we can never predict, with well supported confidence, which current actions will have what future consequences? Whenever you make plans, purporting to learn rationally from the past, are you overestimating your ability to do so?

Other minds

One implication of external world scepticism (in the section, Descartes's dreaming argument) would be your never knowing anything about other people's bodies. *Other minds* scepticism complements that implication. It argues that even if you could escape external world scepticism, thereby knowing about other people's bodies, you would not know that those other bodies have 'inner' mental lives. This is a startling denial, bearing significantly upon how we should live. If it is correct, is there less moral momentum for us to treat each other considerately? If no one can ever know that another human body feels pain, is there no moral need for us to avoid inflicting pain upon others?

Other minds scepticism's basic idea is as follows:

> Imagine walking along a city street. Suddenly, in front of you, someone is writhing on the ground, apparently bleeding. You rush to help, believing that the person is in pain. But do you know that you are not rushing to help someone who does not need it? Might that human being be merely a 'life-like' automaton or zombie – unfeeling, unthinking? Do you know that he or she is not feigning those feelings, playing a dramatic role as a piece of 'performance art'? ('All right. Where's the hidden camera? Am I on TV?') This sort of problem afflicts you – less dramatically – on almost every day of your life. No matter what you observe other human beings to be doing or saying, there is a possibility of their having no such accompanying thoughts or feelings. (Is looking and sounding like a person not enough for *being* a person?)

You cannot simply observe whether or not someone is in pain, for example, because you cannot literally see or hear another's pain. You need to reason, not only observe, if you are to know of their pain. Yet once you do begin thinking about what you are observing, you should realise (claims this sceptic) that there is a possibility of your observing an 'empty shell' of a person – someone who speaks and acts while having no internal mental life. 'Yes, that is possible,' you might say, 'but it is highly unlikely.' However, your confident assessment is supported only by further observations, still of people speaking and acting. No matter how many people you have observed, you have never observed their thoughts and feelings as such. Your powers of reason should accept that there is this possible limitation on your powers of observation.

One popular reply to that other minds scepticism is the *argument from analogy*:

> I observe my behaviour's being like that of other people. And I know that inner thoughts and feelings often accompany my behaviour. By analogy, then, I know that others have such thoughts and feelings accompanying their behaviour. Nature would not have given only me an inner life!

Are there dangers in relying upon this admittedly natural reply to the sceptic? You are merely one instance; and to generalise so broadly from one case – talking about everyone, using just yourself as a basis – is logically questionable. Perhaps it is also metaphysically limiting. For you would evade the sceptic only insofar as you recognise other people acting much as *you* do; and might this leave you unable to understand others as having thoughts or feelings unlike those that you have experienced? Would this be a victory, after all, for the other minds sceptic?

Question 12.6 Could racism or sexism or class prejudice, for example, arise in part because of some unacknowledged other minds scepticism? Might these forms of bigotry be exacerbated by people not really believing that they know various other people – ones who look 'different' or behave 'unusually' – well enough to attribute thoughts and feelings to them? ('They're not much like us. They don't feel in the ways we do. Maybe they don't feel at all.') Can we harm our emotional responses to others by accepting other minds scepticism? Is such scepticism potentially a socially dangerous way of thinking? Or can we accept it purely intellectually, isolating it from our emotional responses?

Being freely rational

Sceptical doubts should make us wonder how well we observe and reason. Are our senses and minds at least somewhat less powerful and free – less 'in control' – than we might wish them to be? Hume's supposed sceptical solution (in the section, Hume on induction) to his inductive scepticism portrays us as thinkers more of habit than inspiration. And though he presented that picture as a solution, maybe a further sceptical worry is implicit in it. Applying it more widely, to other scepticisms too, we might say that it is simply in our *natures* to form those everyday kinds of belief which sceptical arguments conclude are unsupported. That way of speaking could then be thought to imply the following sceptical possibility:

Beliefs which are natural for us could well be *merely* natural – instead of being produced by freely questing rational minds. Our having those beliefs would not prove that we have chosen them wholly freely and rationally (in the sense of their being well supported views); perhaps we have them only because we know no better! It is possible, therefore, that we never believe both wholly freely and wholly rationally.

For instance, external world scepticism argues that your beliefs about your physical surroundings are never knowledge. Nonetheless, it seems, you will continue forming such beliefs; you are unable to stop doing so. You cannot help but believe, within your everyday circumstances, that real cars, roads, walls, and so on, are around you. But is this a mere reflex on your part, something you never freely choose to do? In this respect, are you imprisoned by your nature and circumstances?

It might not feel like that to you: 'I am free to change my mind, to believe in unusual ways. My mind is unfettered.' Is it also wholly rational, though? If so, it is always properly responsive to good evidence (disbelieving what such evidence does not support, and believing what that evidence does support). But then it is not wholly free – because, in effect, it is bound by the evidence. So (concludes this sceptic), your thinking is never both wholly free and wholly rational. To be wholly bound by the quality of one's evidence is to be wholly rational – but not wholly free. And not to be wholly bound in that way is to be somewhat free – but not wholly rational. In one fundamental way or another, therefore, you might not be as you take – and wish – yourself to be. How free is your mind? How rational is it?

Question 12.7   If you were being brainwashed into having various beliefs, would they fail to be knowledge? Even if they were true, would they not be knowledge? If so, is this because someone else would be determining – controlling – what thoughts you have? Must beliefs be freely formed if they are to be knowledge? 'Yes, because otherwise they are not an autonomous thinker's beliefs – and only such a thinker could have knowledge.' Are you such a thinker? How much freedom do you have in believing that it is raining, whenever your eyes and hands make – make? – you believe that it is? Do you have as little mental freedom in that circumstance as you would have if you were being brainwashed to form that belief? Does the world 'control' your mind, to some significant extent?

Moore and commonsense

Few philosophers are sceptics. But is this because they have good objections to the sceptical arguments? Or are they merely believing what they want to believe about our cognitive capacities? 'We are believing what commonsense tells us to believe,' some will say, 'It is plain commonsense not to accept sceptical arguments.'

Perhaps philosophy's best-known instance of that anti-sceptical way of thinking came from the English philosopher G.E. Moore (1873–1958). In a lecture, he held up each of his hands in turn, saying 'Here is one hand, ... and here is another.' From this, he inferred, there are external physical things. And so, he claimed to know, the external world exists! To reject this reasoning (he assured us) would be to favour what is less plausible – sceptical thinking – over what is more plausible – commonsense thinking.

Is commonsense really so powerful a response to sceptics, though? Commonsense beliefs are not obviously what they are because they have battled – and bested – sceptical arguments. They might well have been formed in total ignorance of such reasoning. And if you are accustomed only to commonsense thinking, you might find it hard even to understand sceptical thinking, especially at first.

In any event, most sceptics are not clearly questioning commonsense or everyday views (such as that there is a dog in front of you) in all respects. What they obviously reject is the *less* purely commonsensical thesis that those everyday views are well supported or knowledge. Feel free to retain such views – but (says the sceptic) stop thinking that they are well supported or knowledge! Although commonsense assures you of the dog's presence, you need *more* than commonsense if you are to have detailed, let alone infallible, support for thinking that your commonsense belief that a dog is present is well supported or knowledge. Like anyone, non-philosophers can be confused as to what good support and knowledge even are. (Hopefully, Chapters 8 and 9 have helped us to become clearer on these matters.) So, commonsense by itself does not prove that sceptics are mistaken. Some philosophical engagement with the sceptical arguments might be needed. Even if your belief that a dog is present is patently commonsensical, the claim that you know that a dog is present is at least less transparently commonsensical. This does not make that claim of yours to have knowledge false. Nevertheless, it should spur us to seek further support for the claim.

Question 12.8 Upon being introduced to people, do you believe whatever they tell you about themselves? What would make you begin disbelieving them? Are people instinctively trusting? Yet would that be an intellectually naive instinct? Should we be less trusting, even a little suspicious, in interpreting the world (including what other people tell us)? Are there criteria with which we can know in advance when to doubt someone? Is it possible to achieve a perfect balance between trust and doubt?

Knowing fallibly

Sceptical arguments have bemused and bedevilled philosophers. There is no philosophical agreement on what, if anything, such arguments prove. In this section and the next, I will present two complementary anti-sceptical ideas (ones with applicability to everyday living, too). Let's begin by focussing upon the phenomenon of fallibility.

When characterising knowledge in general, we noted (in Chapter 9 (Fallible knowledge)) the possibility of all or most knowledge being fallible. Since then, we have also wondered, in several specific ways, whether there are underlying limitations on our senses and intellects. Sceptics urge us to fear such limitations. But need we always do so? What we might call the *optimistically* fallibilist response to sceptics says that, rather than proving that we lack knowledge, they really only remind us of some ways in which our knowledge, if present, would be fallible. Having shown the fallibility of the support we have for our views, sceptics infer that those views are never well supported, and hence never knowledge. However, maybe the fallibility is often just part of *how* we know. How could that be so?

Consider this analogy. Imagine denying that anyone can ever be relied upon to be helpful – 'because everyone is fallible in what they do'. This would be like saying that because no one is perfect, no one is even reasonably reliable ('because they could fail *this* time'). The present anti-sceptical suggestion claims that sceptical thinking is – regrettably – that kind of overreaction to our apparent fallibility.

Recall Descartes's external world sceptic, for example (in the section, Descartes's dreaming argument), challenging you in this way:

> You claim to know, via observation, that there is a dog in the room. How do you know that you are not dreaming, rather than observing, its being there?

Here is how a fallibilist about knowledge might reply to that challenge:

> If I am dreaming (in the way described by the sceptic), I am probably being misled about my surroundings. But the sceptic has argued only that I *could* be dreaming, not that I probably am. Now, the fact that I could be misled (by dreaming) about the dog's presence makes me fallible: my belief that there is a dog in the room could fail to be knowledge. This does not prove, however, that my belief *does* fail to be knowledge. If in fact my belief is true and if I am actually seeing the dog, then in fact my belief is knowledge (along the lines described in Chapter 9). It would be fallible knowledge. I would have it – even though, because of my underlying fallibility, I might not have done so. (My belief might not have been knowledge, because it was possible, even with my having those same mental experiences that seem to reveal the dog's presence, for there to be no dog there. I could have been misled without realising it.) Maybe, too, I cannot *prove* that I am seeing, not dreaming, the dog's presence. Yet fallible knowledge – because it is fallible – need not include any such proof. Nonetheless, I could *be* seeing rather than dreaming.

This optimistically fallibilist reply can even admit that the possibility of one's dreaming – not observing – the dog's presence is perennially present: At *any* given time when you seem to be observing the world, it is possible that you are dreaming instead. This never makes what that possibility describes actual, though – more than a possibility. To note a possibility can be to note a mere possibility; what is always possible might never be actual. Consequently, could you be perpetually fallible without perpetually being disturbingly fallible? Yes: fallibility as such is rarely disturbing. (Generally, it is a possibility of falsity. And although actual falsity would be disturbing, the possibility of it is rarely so.) Might you still have much knowledge – with all or most of it happening to be fallible? Yes: fallibility is present throughout your life, meaning that there is a chance of any given one of your beliefs being false, and thereby not being knowledge. But there being a chance of this does not establish its being actually so. On the contrary; there is also the chance that any given belief of yours *is* knowledge. It would simply be fallible knowledge.

If that is possible, then the sceptic has not *proved* that there is no knowledge. Even if (as the sceptic argues) there is an underlying fallibility about our minds, this could coexist with our gaining much knowledge. We need only concede that whatever knowledge we would have is itself fallible. The sceptic must therefore establish more than our fallibility if he or she is to establish our lacking knowledge. Of course, in practice our fallibility does mean that not all of our beliefs are knowledge. Many of them might still be, though. Accordingly, we try to discover which ones are knowledge; and unfortunately our fallibility also means that we often fail in that attempt. So, we do not always *know* which of our views are knowledge. Many of them might nevertheless *be* knowledge.

This is analogous to saying that although our fallibility as agents (people who perform actions) 'hangs over' everything we do, forever making it possible for us to fail on particular occasions of trying to act, we might act competently and successfully, even for sustained periods of time. Although there is fallibility in whatever we do, this does not prove that there is not also reliability. We might well be fallibly reliable! Even so, better that than fallibly unreliable; we should seek, not spurn, that significant level of accomplishment.

Clearly, this section's optimistic fallibilism does not *prove* that we have knowledge. (Nor should we expect it to do so; if at best we have fallible knowledge, then at best we have fallible knowledge that we have knowledge.) But it does explain how it could be much easier for us to have knowledge than sceptics claim. They rightly say that we should never mistake fallibility for infallibility, arrogantly crediting ourselves with the latter. However (concludes this section's anti-sceptical thinking), we should also never mistake fallibility for a constant failure to know. May we thus learn something both from sceptical and from anti-sceptical thinking?

Question 12.9   'If I admit fallibility, I'm admitting doubt – uncertainty. I couldn't live like that. I would have to relinquish all of my beliefs.' Is it really so difficult to admit that few, if any, of one's beliefs are certain – unable to be doubted? Is an admission of fallibility not a doubt as such anyway? Is it just an admission of openness to doubt? Should it be only an admission of openness to serious or rational or somewhat supported doubt? 'But all ways of doubting a view's truth are equally good.' Aren't some doubts deep and dangerous – with some being shallow and harmless?

Improved knowledge

In Chapter 9 (Gradualism), we asked whether there could be *grades* of knowledge – that is, both better and worse knowledge – of a particular fact. That gradualist idea allows us to enrich the previous section's (Knowing fallibly) more standard suggestion that sceptics overreact to our mere fallibility.

Here is how a gradualist about knowledge might encourage you to react to Descartes's dreaming argument, for example:

> My knowing that I am not dreaming is only one of the many possible pieces of evidence with which I might support my belief that a dog is in front of me. So, there remains the chance of my knowing reasonably well, in a normal way, that a dog is present. I would do this on the basis of other evidence – normal observational evidence. If you insist that I must think about whether I am dreaming, then you are expecting me to have much better evidence – special and somewhat philosophical evidence. That would be appropriate if I were to need an especially good grade of knowledge (such as infallible knowledge). But I have no such need. In theory, I can know in a normal way of the dog's presence – even while lacking a much *better* grade of knowledge that a dog is present. My observational evidence could be good, even if it might also have been better.

The previous section suggested that most knowledge would only ever be fallible. This section adds gradualism to that fallibilism. It says that when knowledge of a fact is fallible, in principle that knowledge could be improved. This might occur by improving one's evidence. But improvement's being *possible* does not prove that it *must* occur if knowledge is to be present. Knowledge of a fact could be good – without being even better. There are different possible grades of fallibility in one's support for a particular view: always, your evidence in support of a view is more or less supportive – more or less good. Correlatively, there can be grades in one's knowledge of a particular fact: always, your knowledge of a fact is more or less fallible – more or less good. 'Normal' knowledge of a fact is knowledge of it, for instance, even if in theory there could be better knowledge of it – perhaps such knowledge as philosophers seek of it!

Question 12.10   Can improving as a person include improving one's knowledge of particular facts? Could you know that torture is cruel – and then improve this knowledge? (And will this make you a better person, other things being equal?) Would you improve that knowledge if you were to begin *feeling* it more deeply? Might you improve that knowledge by coming to know more about the bodily or psychological effects of torture on its victims? Would it be immoral of you to approve of people being tortured, even if you were not to know perfectly – that is, unimprovably well – that they feel pain?

What you are

Sceptical doubts are at the heart of epistemology. Regardless of whether you become a sceptic, you have not fully engaged with philosophical thinking about knowledge if you have never taken sceptical doubts seriously. Pursuing such epistemological thinking, however, also deepens your immersion in those metaphysical issues with which this book began. If a sceptic is right to deny you knowledge of an external world, for example, this is not only an epistemological result about you. It is a fundamental metaphysical feature of you, helping to make you whatever kind of being you are. The same is true if that sceptic is mistaken. If you have knowledge of an external world, but it is always fallible, say, then this, too, is a fundamental metaphysical aspect of you, contributing to your being whatever kind of being you are.

This book commenced by asking what kind of thing you are. It ends with that same question. Now, though, we can ask it with a stronger sense of the depth and subtlety lurking within it. For now we see how what we *are* is partly a matter of what and how and whether we *know* – and vice versa. Are we thus essentially rational, at least in this way? Is it essential to your being a person that you can know much about the physical world, for example? And is that easier if you are wholly physical yourself? Is it essential, if you are to be a person, that you can know of other people's having minds? And is that easier if they are wholly physical themselves? Is part of being a person the possession of a fully rational mind, able to think wholly freely? And is this easier if people are not physical? In these and kindred ways, what a person is affects how, if at all, a person knows; and how, if at all, a person knows is part of what a person is. Ultimately, the questions in this book are interlocked. What are we? Are we what can know?

And if we can know, *what* can we know? Can we know what properties we have? Can we know what properties the rest of the world has? Can we know what properties we *could* have, given what ones we already have and what ones the rest of the world has? That would be no small feat. Most of us most of the time, I fear, have at best poor knowledge of what we are, let alone of what we could be like. But philosophy is one means of gaining – then improving – such knowledge of people. It is also thereby one means of improving oneself as a person. Does that make it important? Yes.

Further reading

On scepticism in general:

A.J. Ayer, *The Problem of Knowledge* (London: Macmillan, 1956), ch. 2.

Myles Burnyeat (ed.), *The Skeptical Tradition* (Berkeley, CA: University of California Press, 1983).

Keith DeRose and Ted A. Warfield (eds), *Skepticism: A Contemporary Reader* (New York: Oxford University Press, 1999).

Stephen Cade Hetherington, *Knowledge Puzzles: An Introduction to Epistemology* (Boulder, CO: Westview Press, 1996), chs 18–27.

Nicholas Rescher, *Scepticism: A Critical Reappraisal* (Oxford: Blackwell, 1980).

Barry Stroud, *The Significance of Philosophical Scepticism* (Oxford: Clarendon Press, 1984).

For Descartes's sceptical doubts:

René Descartes, *Meditations on First Philosophy*, I.

For Hume's scepticism about induction:

David Hume, *An Enquiry Concerning Human Understanding*, secs IV, V.

On other minds scepticism:

Alec Hyslop, *Other Minds* (Dordrecht: Kluwer, 1995).

For Moore's response to scepticism:

G.E. Moore, *Philosophical Papers* (London: George Allen & Unwin, 1959), ch. VII.

On scepticism and thinking freely:

Christopher Hookway, *Scepticism* (London: Routledge, 1990), chs VII, VIII.

On scepticism and fallibility and improved knowledge:

Stephen Hetherington, *Good Knowledge, Bad Knowledge: On Two Dogmas of Epistemology* (Oxford: Clarendon Press, 2001), ch. 2.

Index